Made in Bristol

50 STORIES OF LOCAL ENTERPRISE AND INVENTION

This book is about 50 products, some well-known, some practically unknown, some unexpected and a few downright odd. But they all have one important thing in common: they are, or were, made in Bristol.

This selection is purely personal. The descriptions and stories focus on the products themselves and the people who invented and made them. They do not include lengthy histories of the companies concerned. If occasionally I let my own prejudices intrude, I make no apology. This is not intended to be a scholarly work for serious local historians but an entertaining book for the general reader who wants to be informed, amused and sometimes amazed. It is also for the people who worked, or are still working, for the companies featured.

It should also be said that the featured companies were not necessarily the only Bristol manufacturers of that particular product.

I have inevitably had to omit many products – but the people of Bristol have produced such an amazing variety of things over the years that it is clearly impossible to include everything in one book.

David Bolton, October 2011

Made in Bristol

50 STORIES OF LOCAL ENTERPRISE AND INVENTION

David Bolton

First published in 2011 by Redcliffe Press Ltd.,
81g Pembroke Road, Bristol BS8 3EA

E: info@redcliffepress.co.uk
www.redcliffepress.co.uk

ISBN 978-1-904537-91-5

British Library Cataloguing-in-Publication Data
A catalogue record for this book is available from the British Library

Design and typesetting by Stephen Morris www.stephen-morris.co.uk
Printed and bound in the UK by Hobbs the Printers Ltd, Totton, Hampshire

Contents

BEER

George's Brewery and the Bristol Beer Factory

IN YEARS GONE BY, most English people drank huge quantities of beer, often as much as a gallon a day. There was a very good reason for this. It was probably better for them than the local drinking water, which was often heavily contaminated. By the start of the eighteenth century one French writer remarked 'more grain is consumed in England for making beer than for baking bread'. Contributing to this was the fact that strong beer was not much more expensive than water. A gallon in an ale house cost only 5d (2p decimal equivalent) or 1p for home consumption. As a result, most English families, including children, drank beer for breakfast, lunch and dinner.

Bristolians were no exception. In the seventeenth century there were small local breweries all over the city, many of them attached to its 600 or so pubs. The biggest and most successful of these breweries was close to Bristol Bridge, named the Bristol Brewery by John Hawkins, its somewhat unimaginative owner. By 1702 he had become so wealthy and influential that he was Sir John Hawkins, the Mayor of Bristol. In 1788 the Bristol Brewery was taken over by Philip George and renamed George's. Over the next two hundred years George's Brewery ruthlessly bought up and closed down dozens of smaller competing companies. Typical of these was the Ashton Gate Brewery, which had been so successful that by the early 1930s it was brewing enough beer to supply its own chain of 120 pubs, extending from Pontypool to Bridgwater. George's obviously could not tolerate such an upstart competitor, so in 1933 they bought the Ashton Gate company and promptly closed it down, retaining only one of its brands, Milk Stout. As a result, George's now owned around 1,200 pubs throughout the South West, and its output increased to 250,000 barrels a year and 100,000 bottles a day. The policy of aggressive acquisitions was repeated in 1956 when George's took over its last remaining serious competitor, Bristol United Breweries, and thus became by far the biggest brewery in the region.

The brewing industry has always had a 'dog eat dog', or rather big dog eat smaller dog, tendency, and George's finally got its comeuppance when it was in turn taken over by Courage in 1961. The brewery, still on the same site next to Bristol Bridge, was then sold to Imperial Tobacco, which itself was taken over by the Hanson Trust, which in turn sold it to the Australian brewers Elders IXL in 1986 and ultimately to Scottish and Newcastle. Sadly, reflecting its name, this

George's brewery
from Bristol Bridge
in 1920
(Photo: brizzlebornand
bred)

last company had little sentimental attachment to Bristol and in May 1999, despite promises to the contrary, the decision was taken to close down the brewery after 297 years. As a result, in October of that year the familiar smell of fermenting hops and barley which wafted over Castle Park into Broadmead and then all over central Bristol, was suddenly no more. A local historian, like thousands of Bristolians, noticed the difference: 'It was George's brewery which provided the most dominant of the city smells, and the one that was around the longest. When George's – and later Courage's – were brewing, that was Bristol's last real big smell. When the brewery closed down, it was like putting a light out. The city is just not the same.'

Seventy-one people lost their jobs as a result of the closure. In the words of their local union leader, 'the brewery was a treasured part of the Bristol landscape'. The site, which extended to a million square feet, was sold off to developers and most of the buildings were demolished. It is now taking shape as one of central Bristol's umpteen developments of offices, shops, bars and 'luxurious waterside apartments', as they like to call them.

This pattern of seemingly relentless takeovers and amalgamations has resulted in the extraordinary situation in which today more than 80 per cent of all beer drunk in this country comes from just four, foreign-owned, brewers: Carlsberg, Heineken, Coors and Inbev. But all is not doom and gloom. Former prime minister Gordon Brown, when he was chancellor, earned himself the title 'beer drinkers' champion' when he offered a glimmer of hope to British brewers. In his 2004 budget he announced that the first 60,000 hectolitres of beer – that's just over 10.5

The Grain Barge, moored by the side of the Hotwell Road, flagship of the Bristol Beer Factory

million pints – produced by any one brewery would attract only half the normal duty. Perhaps because the big brewers, or the beerage as they are sometimes known, have traditionally been generous supporters of the Conservative party, he had decided to encourage much smaller competitors.

His announcement opened the door for small, independent brewers, and one of the micro-breweries that seized the opportunity was the Bristol Beer Factory, which produces beer on the site of the old Ashton Gate Brewery. It started in 2003 when George Ferguson, the locally based architect, ex-Lord Lieutenant of Bristol, columnist in the *Evening Post* and incorrigible wearer of red trousers, happened to hear that an old brewery building less than 100 metres from his Tobacco Factory theatre and bar complex in Bedminster was for sale. (Ribena was produced there in the 1940s, as you will see later in this book.) George Ferguson employed an expert brewery engineer, Simon Bartlett, to install the necessary plant, and in 2004 the Bristol Beer Factory produced its first pint. It was helped by the sad demise of another well known Bristol micro-brewery, Smiles, in 2005; master brewer Chris Thurgeson was made redundant by Smiles one Friday and started at the Bristol Beer Factory the following Monday.

Since then the company has grown slowly but surely. The publicity for some of its beers could be lifted from a wine critic's column in one of the broadsheets. How about this description of No 7 Traditional Best Bitter? 'Its toffee malt flavours are balanced with smooth hop bitterness and aroma.' Or this for its Sun Rise brew, a

Milk Stout brewed by the Ashton Gate Brewery Company and its modern reincarnation brewed by the Bristol Beer Factory

right: a selection of beers brewed by the Bristol Beer Factory

name coined by the original Ashton Gate Brewery: 'A refreshing Golden Ale with a slight biscuity malt taste and strong citrus hop aroma.' One of its best-selling brands is called simply Red, a sly reference to George Ferguson's trousers. But when it comes to describing the strongest beer, Gold, the blurb writers are more to the point: 'It will do what 5 per cent ales are required to do!' Enough said.

The economics of brewing beer can be simplified to absolute basics: one-third raw materials, one-third production costs and one-third duty. The resulting pint is then sold to the pub or bar for approximately 80p, and the price is then marked up by anything up to 400 per cent. At present the Bristol Beer Factory produces forty brewer's barrels of beer a week or, in layman's language, just under twelve thousand pints, and it could make more. These people might be relative beginners, but they clearly know what they are doing. In 2009 their Milk Stout was awarded Gold in its category by CAMRA, the Campaign for Real Ale. As Simon Bartlett rather modestly responded, 'I knew it was good but I didn't know it was that bloody good.'

You can sample the Bristol Beer Factory's brews in a number of local watering holes and especially on board its flagship, the Grain Barge, which is moored on the Hotwell Road more or less opposite the ss *Great Britain* and just across the docks from where it was built in Charles Hill's shipyard in 1936. According to the company's website, the Beer Factory 'is keeping one of Bristol's most historical industries alive'. Adspeak it might be, but in a small way it happens also to be true.

BIRD SEED

Made by Capern's

NOT LONG AGO, if you asked almost any owner of a budgerigar, parrot or canary what bird seed they bought, the answer was invariably 'Capern's, of course'. The two seemed to go together like Branston and pickle or Kellogg's and cornflakes. But if you had asked those same people where Capern's bird seed came from, very few would have answered 'Bristol'.

An enamel Capern's advertisement from the 1920s

Francis Capern, or Fred as he was usually known, came originally from Weston-super-Mare, where he had a small chemist's shop. He was also keen on birds, both wild and caged, and it was this interest that eventually made his name. His bird food business really started when customers in his shop asked for advice about what to feed their birds, especially those that clearly were not feeling too well. From observing his own feathered friends, he came to the conclusion that dusty, musty and probably dirty seeds did not do them much good. He suggested instead a balanced diet of various seeds which had been specially cleaned and put in bags, which he sold in his chemist's shop. It was not long before more people came in to buy bird food than pills and potions for humans, and it was from these small beginnings that Fred Capern eventually made his fortune.

He founded his bird seed company in 1879, the same year he married the splendidly named Mercy Morgan. He was also sensible enough to move to Bristol in the same year. There business boomed, and before long the House of Capern sold more than 50 specialised products with exotic names such as Capern's Seed and Fruit Mixture with Egg-flakes, Finch Mixture, Refresher for Finches and Linnets, New Food for Black Birds and Thrushes, Budgerigar Mixture and Foreign Finch Mixture. He even developed a nice little sideline in medicines for birds, with names like Bird Tonic and Canary-Anodyne for Chills and Colds. Capern's factory started out in a small building in Charles Street, just off Stokes Croft; this was probably the world's first bird food factory. By 1896 these premises were too cramped and Fred moved to an old sugar warehouse, built in 1728, in Lewin's Mead. There his business stayed for the next 50 years, although the building changed in appearance from a warehouse to a large Georgian house when it was given a rather grandiose façade and porch. In his spare time Fred Capern also found time to write *Capern's Bird Book*, which its publishers claimed was 'interesting and informative to all lovers of pet birds, invaluable to the experienced fancier, indispensable to the amateur'. Fred retired in 1910 and shortly before his death in 1914 he gave away a large part of his fortune: £45,000 went to the Bristol Royal Infirmary and another £45,000 to Bristol General Hospital, where the directors

Capern's Bird Food factory in Lewins Mead; now the Hotel du Vin

acknowledged his generosity by naming a ward after him. The man who took over his business, Bristolian Harry Jenkins, made another fortune out of sanded sheets used to line the floors of bird cages.

In the 1920s the business continued to do well, partly because of the catchy slogan 'The seed with the song in it'. But then, in 1934, as so often happens, a successful local business was taken over by a big national company, in this case Spratt's, manufacturers of dog food and dog biscuits; and in the spirit of dog eat dog, Spratt's were in turn taken over by Spillers. In 1956 the Capern's factory finally moved out of the centre of Bristol to a new plant in Yatton, designed by the well known Bristol architects Alec French and Partners and costing £150,000. There, 140 people were employed in cleaning and blending hundreds of tons of seeds from all over the world, and then filling, weighing and sealing them in 120 packets a minute. The factory even had its own railway siding connected to the main line. The brand continued to sell well, partly because of a TV advertising campaign which ran for two years. It starred a talking budgie called Sparkie Williams that was taught to say seven different, but all very positive, things about Capern's seeds. He became a national celebrity but eventually fell off his perch and is now in a museum in Newcastle-upon-Tyne, suitably stuffed. Eventually, in 1988, Bob Martin's, the company that seems to have a product to suit your pet's every need, decided that Capern's bird seeds would fit very nicely into its product range. The factory in Yatton still employs 120 people, but unfortunately Fred Capern's name has all but disappeared.

As for the old factory in Lewin's Mead, the building became an electrical wholesalers and was then left derelict until it was eventually restored and transformed, at a cost of £4.5 million, into an exceedingly smart 40-room hotel and restaurant with the appropriately smart-sounding French name of Hotel du Vin.

Sparkie Williams, stuffed and on display in a museum in Newcastle

BLUE GLASS

Made by Isaac Jacobs

BRISTOL WAS FAMOUS for its glassmaking industry long before Bristol Blue Glass was first manufactured. The city's skyline was once dotted with all-brick conical glassmaking furnaces. In the eighteenth century more than 60 glasshouses made over half the bottles and window glass in Britain, and a contemporary writer commented: 'The city contains as many glasshouses as churches.' It was a dirty industry even by the standards of those times. Daniel Defoe wrote of: 'The city, from the continual smoke arising from them, being constantly darkened and in dirt, while the inhabitants are almost suffocated with noxious effluvia.' That was a visitor's description. For the glassmakers themselves, conditions were horrendous, and when the Bristol philanthropist Hannah More was brave enough to enter a glassworks, she was horrified. 'The swearing, eating and drinking of these half-dressed, black-looking beings gave a most infernal and horrid appearance,' she wrote. 'They themselves mockingly called it Botany Bay or Living Hell.' Another observer, John Eyres, was more shocked by the eating habits of the glassmakers: 'They eat snails, partly as a delicacy and partly to combat chest diseases. They are baked upon a shovel, held for a few minutes at the mouth of the furnace and then taken from their shells with a two-inch nail.'

Nowadays the remnants of only one of these furnaces are left. It was built in the 1780s and at 120 feet high was the tallest in the city. Today it is just a stump that has been transformed into a restaurant at the back of the Ramada Plaza hotel, next to St Mary Redcliffe church. Defoe and Hannah More would not recognise it, and neither would those who regarded it as a living hell.

The story of Bristol Blue Glass started towards the end of the eighteenth century. Richard Champion, a merchant and potter specialising in fine white porcelain, went into business with a chemist, William Cookworthy. The two of them decided that they needed a steady supply of good quality cobalt oxide to give a deep blue glaze decoration to their milky white porcelain. Cookworthy went in search of it, and in 1763 he gained exclusive import rights to all the cobalt oxide colouring agent, known as smalt, from the Royal Saxon Cobalt Works in Saxony. He of course used it in the company he owned with Champion, but he also sold it on at a considerable profit to a number of glassmakers in Bristol and other cities.

In the 1780s, Lazarus and Isaac Jacobs emerged as the most famous makers of Bristol Blue Glass. Lazarus was a Jewish immigrant who came from Frankfurt in Germany some time between 1755 and 1760. By 1763 he was sufficiently estab-lished in the glassmaking business to commission a local painter, Michael Edkins,

The remains of a glass-making furnace near St Mary Redcliffe church

to decorate decanters and glasses with gilding. Like many first-generation immigrants, Lazarus Jacobs worked hard, and in 1774 he took over the bankrupt Perrot Glassworks and two adjoining houses in Temple Street. There, with his 16-year-old son Isaac, he revived the business and established a reputation as a flint glass cutter. The company did well, specialising in decorating blue glass in particular: the combination of high-quality blue cobalt from Saxony and the recently invented flint glass, or lead crystal as it is now called, resulted in glassware of outstanding quality. Part of the company's profits went into building a new synagogue on Temple Street in 1786. A year later, Lazarus, his family and business moved to Avon Street, where the company was renamed the Non-Such Flint Glass Manufactory. By this time it was making, cutting, engraving and decorating glass on a relatively large scale.

Lazarus died in 1796, aged 87, and his son Isaac took over. He was just as energetic and businesslike as his father, and three years later he had made enough money to buy a large house in the fashionable suburb of Kingsdown. He announced that his company would 'continue manufacturing items in the Glass Line (even the most common articles) of that superior quality which has hitherto given him the decided preference to any other House in the Kingdom'. Isaac clearly had considerable chutzpah, but perhaps he was fortunate that there was no Advertising Standards Authority in those days. In 1806 one of his advertisements mentioned 'specimens of the Dessert (set) which I Jacobs had the honour of sending to Her Majesty', and apparently this was enough for him to claim that he was 'Glass manufacturer to His Majesty', even though there is no evidence that his gift was even acknowledged. His advertisements went on to claim that he 'made glass for Europe's aristocracy'; and to cap it all, in 1812, the Jacobs family was granted its own coat-of-arms. Unhappily, the good times did not last. The

Glass blowing at Bristol Blue Glass South West, Bedminster

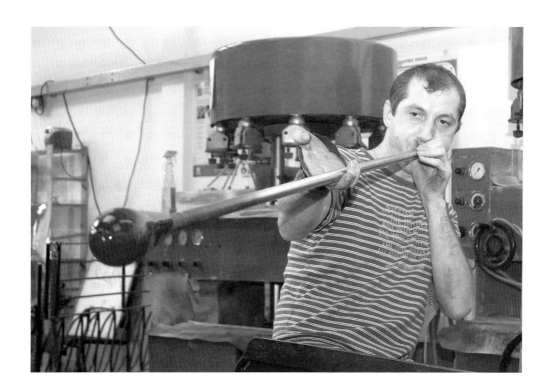

Napoleonic Wars were disastrous for trade, Isaac sank up to his ears in debt and in 1820 his business finally failed. Isaac Jacobs was declared bankrupt and imprisoned, although only for a token two days.

Nowadays, original pieces of Bristol Blue Glass, particularly those with Isaac's signature, can fetch thousands of pounds at auction. It is said, however, that unless you are a specialist, it is sometimes difficult to tell whether some pieces are the real thing or not. Blue glass was manufactured in Liverpool, for example. That said, experts maintain that authentic Bristol Blue Glass has a deeper colour and what has been described as 'an oily, satiny feel' to it.

During the latter part of the nineteenth century, glassmaking in the city went into decline, and in 1922 the last traditional Bristol glasshouse closed its doors. Nowadays however two rival companies, called rather confusingly Bristol Blue Glass Ltd in Brislington and Bristol Blue Glass South West in Bedminster, carry on the tradition. Interestingly the latter company has recently moved to where there was a flint glass house as long ago as 1730. On the site now there is a busy glass works with daily glass blowing demonstrations using two huge, and very hot, furnaces. There is also a glass museum containing over 140 glass items, some dating back to the second and third centuries. The exhibition includes a fine signed piece of original Bristol Blue Glass produced by Isaac Jacobs. The blue glass pieces which you can watch being made there may well be collectable but regrettably never as valuable as the original pieces made by Isaac Jacobs that started it all.

BOOTS

Made by G B Britton and Sons

GEORGE BRYANT BRITTON WAS BORN IN 1857. He left school early to work as a cobbler, and with the Kingswood collieries near-by, there were always plenty of boots to repair. Then, in the mid-1870s, he started a small boot-making business in Kingswood. Less than three years later the capital worth of the company had reached a considerable £1,100, and when a partner, George Jefferies, joined him in 1880, the two invested in a new factory in Waters Road. The company installed 20 sewing machines and three presses for cutting soles, all treadle-operated, and before long it employed more than 50 people plus a large number of outworkers. The latter were notoriously badly paid, and in the 1880s and 1890s there were many houses in Kingswood with their lights on all night as the workers struggled to make a living. Average weekly earnings at this time amounted to only 3s 6d, about £14 today, which was partly as a result of the weakness of the unions in the Kingswood area compared with those in central Bristol.

George Bryant Britton

After Jefferies retired, George Britton carried on and in 1899 opened a new, much larger factory in Lodge Road, Kingswood, employing more than 150 workers. During the early 1900s his sons George Ewart and Samuel Wesley joined the business, and the factory was extended. The firm specialised in hob-nailed boots, first with the name Dryfoot and then Welshod, made especially for the miners of the Kingswood and South Wales collieries. Output rose to nearly 6,000

Lodge Road factory, Kingswood, 1968: a picture giving a sense of the scale of production

pairs a week, and at the outbreak of the First World War the company received massive government orders for army boots. For the next four years the factory worked flat out from 6.30 a.m. until 9.30 p.m., making hundreds of thousands of boots for the men in the trenches of northern France. The factory only closed at 9.30 so that 'the men could refresh themselves with a pint of beer or two before going home'. Britton's net profits tripled; as always, war, for some people at least, was no bad thing.

George Britton died of a heart attack in July, 1929 at the age of 72, soon after attending a meeting of the National Federation of Shoemakers. He had been a tough, energetic, hard-working man who never lost his broad local accent. He spent a lot of time on the factory floor in his shirt sleeves telling his employees, all of whom he knew by name, how the job should be done. In addition to being a wealthy industrialist he was also a JP for 24 years and simultaneously both Lord Mayor of Bristol and Member of Parliament for the East division of the city.

In his old age he mellowed and was regarded as 'a lovely man' by many. Joyce Storey, in her autobiography *The House in South Road*, remembers in the late 1920s being allowed into the garden of his big house in Lodge Causeway: 'It was like a fairyland, with rose gardens and bowers and unusual trees… Mr Britton patted my head and presented me with a perfect white rose and told me that his wife adored roses and that all the roses in the garden were hers. On the spur of the moment I asked him if I could come and sit in his garden again, and he said quietly that I could come any time I liked.'

During the 1930s the firm contracted; weekly output of boots between 1930 and 1934 averaged only 2,500 pairs. But G B Britton and Sons survived, just, until the Second World War again heralded a return to full production and big profits, averaging £22,250 a year. Between 1941 and 1945 the company worked round the clock once more, producing hundreds of thousands of army boots, even though production had to be moved temporarily from Lodge Road so that the factory could be turned over to aircraft component and repair work.

After the war it was the same old story of decline until Britton's fortuitously bought four boot-making machines from C and J Clark of Somerset. Clark's had acquired from the Barcelona businessman Gonzalo Mediano the world rights to a new direct-moulding process in which rubber soles and heels were moulded, vulcanised and bonded to leather uppers in one operation. The traditional bootmakers of Kingswood were appalled, but in 1955, as a result of secret experiments with the Clark's machines in a partitioned-off corner of the factory, the Tuf boot was invented. It was a light, flexible, waterproof, comfortable but tough working man's boot, and with the help of television advertising it became so popular that at one time more than 70,000 pairs a week were being made. The Tuf boot was followed by the Gluv shoe. Both products were sold with an unconditional six-month guarantee. Britton's payroll rose from 450 in 1951 to more than 3,000 in 1968, and between 1955 and 1965 weekly output soared to 120,000 pairs of boots and shoes a week; profits rose tenfold.

It could not last. By the end of the 1960s complacency and cheap foreign imports led to big losses. Jack Britton, George's grandson, retired, and no follow-up to the highly successful Tuf boot was invented. The company went into a long, painful decline. In 1975, Britton's became a subsidiary of Ward White Ltd of Northampton; by 1985 the workforce had fallen to 750, and by 2001 it had shrunk to 130. Four days before Christmas that year the last boots made in Bristol came off the production line, and the doors closed for the last time. In the words of the local union leader: 'Britton's was more like a community than a factory, but it was impossible to compete. They could have worked for nothing and still it would have been 20 per cent cheaper to make the goods in Asia.' In 2002 the factory was demolished and the site, like its owner's house, is now a housing estate. George Bryant Britton is probably turning in his grave.

5　BOXKITE

Made by the British and Colonial Aeroplane Company

Sir George White

An early advert for the Zodiac, the plane that never flew

THE BOXKITE WAS THE AIRCRAFT that really started Bristol's aircraft industry, and Sir George White was the man who got it off the ground. He was a notable Bristolian, born in Cotham in 1854, the son of a painter and decorator who became a solicitor's clerk and then a stockbroker. Knighted in 1904, he has been described as 'a dapper little Edwardian, fierce in manner, with tireless energy and a "take-over outlook" in business affairs'. After he made a fortune from playing the stock exchange he invested a lot of the money in Bristol's first trams and buses, and as a result he virtually invented commuting in the area.

In the summer of 1909, George White was on holiday in the south of France, recovering from an illness, when he saw an advertisement for a flying display. Intrigued, he went along and watched Wilbur Wright flying one of his first aircraft. George White was so impressed that he immediately cabled his brother Samuel back in Bristol with the message: 'We must start an aircraft company'. With typical impatience he almost immediately negotiated a deal to build under licence a French aeroplane, the Zodiac, back in Bristol. The French at that time were far in advance of the British, who persisted in regarding aeroplanes as mere toys for the idle rich. Significantly it was a Frenchman, Louis Blériot, in a French aircraft, who first flew across the English Channel in July, 1909 and won a prize of £1,000 from the *Daily Mail*.

The factory Sir George White chose for his newly-formed British and Colonial Aeroplane Company was a pair of unimpressive corrugated iron tram sheds in Filton, a Gloucestershire village with a population at the time of no more than 500. At a meeting of the Bristol Tramways Company shareholders, Sir George, as chairman, announced the change of use, justifying it by saying the new-fangled aeroplanes he was going to produce would attract many more passengers to the recently extended tram route from Horfield. The shareholders were placated, but unfortunately Sir George's first aeroplane was a total flop. The Zodiac made in Filton stubbornly refused to leave the ground, probably because it was too heavy for the very limited power its engine produced, and the French test pilot Maurice Edmond recommended that it should be pushed into a corner and forgotten. George White followed his advice and managed to extract 15,000 francs in compensation from the French company. Miraculously, only three weeks later, on July 30, 1910, the Bristol Challenger Biplane, as it was officially called, made its maiden flight. Because of its extraordinary appearance it soon became better known simply as the Bristol Boxkite.

M. Tétard in Flight Over Clifton Suspension Bridge No. 6

This first aeroplane was built with such amazing speed because it was based very closely on a French design, the Farman Biplane, which had appeared in various aeroplane magazines of the time. It was not quite a straight copy; it had one or two minor modifications and improvements devised by the chief engineer of the new company, George Challenger, who in a previous incarnation had been foreman of Sir George White's bus works. The Farman brothers complained, with some justification, that their patents had been infringed and took George White to court, but he argued that his modifications meant it was practically a different aircraft, and he won his case. The aeroplane was an unlovely contraption made of wooden stays, steel cables and two pairs of wings of stretched canvas. The under-carriage was a pair of what looked like wheels from a moped with wooden skids. The whole device was only 38 feet long and had a wingspan of 46 feet, but with a French Gnome engine producing only 49 horsepower, it was hardly going to break any speed records even then. Its maximum was 45 knots (about 51 mph). A contemporary report confirmed that 'very little harm could come to one's person travelling at such a velocity'. When it was announced that Maurice Edmond would pilot the plane on its maiden flight on Salisbury Plain, sceptical spectators lay flat on the ground when it prepared for take-off, because they simply did not believe it would fly. They were hoping at most to glimpse a few inches of daylight between the flying machine and the ground, and were flabbergasted when it rose to 150 feet. Shortly after that Edmond flew the aircraft to Bristol, and after an emergency

Monsieur Tétard at the controls over the Avon Gorge

The Boxkite takes off from Clifton Downs, November 1910

landing in the marshalling yard of Bath's Green Park railway station, he landed it on the lawn behind Filton House, much to Sir George White's amazement.

On November 12, 1910 the company arranged an historic publicity stunt on Durdham Downs. A tent hangar was erected and a well-known French pilot, Maurice Tétard, was hired to make a demonstration flight. *The Bristol Times and Mirror* of November 14, 1910 reported:

> After his fine flight, Maurice Tétard was interviewed. He does not speak English but in voluble French, accompanied by many gestures, he expressed his delight at the behaviour of the Bristol Biplane. It was the first time he had been up in a machine of that make and it was certainly the best he had ever flown. The flight was exceptionally difficult because of the tricky wind prevailing. On the ground the wind was not particularly heavy though gusty, but in the upper air he struck many whirlwinds coming from the Avon Gorge. The effect was to suck him downwards, and this prevented him from attaining any great elevation.

This is a phenomenon experienced by many hot air balloonists, and it is interesting to speculate what would have happened to Bristol's embryonic aircraft industry had the plane crashed.

Sir George White was a salesman as well as a businessman. Soon after this successful demonstration flight he arranged for one of his aircraft to fly to military manoeuvres taking place on Salisbury Plain which was in effect a very early air show. The Boxkite proved its potential in an aerial reconnaissance role, and a month later the company received its first order, for eight aircraft, although strangely it was from the Russian, rather than the British, government. To train pilots to fly the new aircraft, the company opened its own flying school at Larkhill on Salisbury Plain. The chief flying instructor was Collyns Pizey, once an apprentice at Bristol Tramways. By the end of 1913, some 150 Bristol Boxkites had been produced, 200 people were employed and the British and Colonial Aeroplane Company was unquestionably up and flying. When the workaholic and chain-smoking Sir George White died three years later, aged 62, Bristol was already on the world aviation map and destined to remain there.

Although none of the original aircraft has survived, a replica can be seen hanging from the ceiling of the City Museum in Queen's Road, one of three used in the 1960s film *Those Magnificent Men in their Flying Machines*. It was particularly high-profile in 2010, when the centenary of Sir George White's first venture into powered flight was marked by an exhibition in the museum. It is fitting that the Bristol Boxkite is on permanent display since this aircraft really marked the beginning of Bristol's aircraft industry.

THE BRABAZON

Made by the Bristol Aeroplane Company

THE BRABAZON WAS PROBABLY the biggest white elephant in the history of British aviation – and there have been plenty. The idea was first proposed in 1943 by a cabinet committee chaired by Lord Brabazon, who had been Minister of Aircraft Production in Churchill's government. The committee decided that after the war Britain would need a big transatlantic airliner to compete with those made by such American companies as Lockheed and Boeing. The Bristol Aeroplane Company had an advantage when it came to such a giant aircraft because in 1937 it had started design work on a super-heavy bomber, dubbed by the company the Hundred-Ton Bomber. These designs were dusted off and modified, not least by fitting the new Bristol Centaurus 18-cylinder radial engine. In November 1944 the company's plans were made public and the government gave them the go-ahead on condition that they would not interfere with work on military aircraft. The construction of the first prototype started in October 1945, while the monster assembly hall was still under construction.

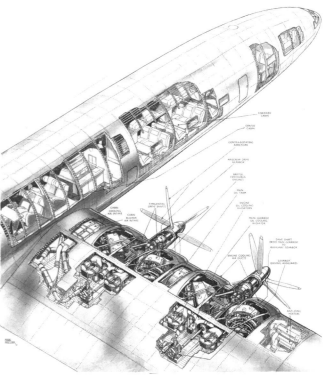

The luxurious accommodation

Development took much longer than expected because in many respects it was new technology. For a start, the fuselage had a fully stressed skin and was fully pressurised, the passenger cabin was air conditioned, the flight controls were hydraulically powered and, above all, it was an enormous aircraft. According to the company publicity at the time:

> It is not just another big aircraft – it is the biggest aircraft yet built in this country and larger than anything that has yet flown in the world.

Its fuselage was 177 feet (53.9 m) long and the wing span a massive 230 feet (70.1 m), which is 35 feet wider than Boeing's much later 747 Jumbo; the tail fin was as high as four double-decker buses.

The Brabazon's eight engines were buried deep in the wings to reduce drag, and they drove eight enormous propellers. Even with all this power, however, the Brabazon's maximum cruising speed was only 260 mph, which would mean an Atlantic crossing could take more than 13 hours. Perhaps most unbelievable of all, it was, in spite of its enormous size, designed to carry up to only 150 passengers. This

In flight at the Farnborough Air Show, 1950

Minus its wings outside the specially-built Aircraft Assembly Hall at Filton, 1947

reflected the thinking of the time: flying was only for the very rich and powerful who expected to travel in 'a flying hotel', with accommodation more akin to that provided by the *Queen Elizabeth* and other great transatlantic liners than by an aeroplane. It had private first class cabins, a 32-seat cinema, a dining room, a swish cocktail bar and a luxurious lounge. Each passenger was allotted more than six square metres of space, equivalent to the interior of three modern cars.

Passengers could theoretically take off from London, have a cocktail or two at the bar, then a four-course dinner and perhaps watch a film. Finally, they could retire to bed to be woken nine hours later, just in time for breakfast in New York. The idea that a very large aircraft could make flying cheaper seemed never to have occurred to anyone at the time, at least, not in Britain. Boeing had other ideas...

In order to get this giant into the air, the runway at Filton needed to be reconstructed with concrete to take the plane's massive weight. It also had to be extended from 1,500 yards to 2,750 yards, a move that sadly necessitated the demolition of the village of Charlton, which had the severe misfortune of being situated at the far end of the runway. The village included a pub, the Carpenter's Arms, a post office, a chapel, several farm houses and a manor house. The people of Charlton were promised that their village would be rebuilt, but it never was, and most villagers were rehoused on the new council estate at Patchway. To add insult to injury, the rubble from their houses was used to build the runway extension.

The silver prototype Brabazon took off for the first time from Filton on September 4, 1949. The local media advised people to stay away for fear of massive traffic jams, but they took no notice and more than 20,000 watched as the plane lifted off. The

Manchester Guardian reported the event with this piece of purple prose:

> The beautiful monster took to the air with superb grace and extraordinarily little
> fuss. In the taxiing trials it looked as if even the eternity of the runway was none
> too long. The eye foreshortened it and there were moments when the Brabazon
> looked like a great swan wondering how to take off from a village pond. But at noon
> today it taxied to the western end of the runway – a fire engine scuttling at a discreet
> interval behind it like a nervous beetle – turned and took to the air in about 500
> yards. The ease and unexpectedness of it set even newspapermen cheering.

A few more people watched it on the infant BBC television sevice in one of the corporation's first live outside broadcasts, which was translated into eight languages. For a
short time, Filton and Bristol were world-famous.

When it transpired that the Brabazon needed less than a quarter of the length of
the new runway to take off, the people of Charlton were understandably incensed.
Once airborne, Bill Pegg the chief test pilot was heard to say: 'Good God. It works!'
The plane was in the air for just 27 minutes, taking a leisurely aerial stroll over north
Bristol, Avonmouth and Chipping Sodbury. Afterwards, when Pegg was asked what
it was like to pilot such a monstrous aircraft, he answered: 'It's quite easy. We just fly
the cockpit and the rest of it trails along behind.'

Early test flights went so well that after only three hours' flying time the Brabazon
was taken to the Farnborough Air Show before droning her way over the south coast

seaside resorts to give taxpayers a sight of what their money had paid for. But from then on it was all downhill. Four years of test flights and modifications followed, but even after 400 hours' flying time the aircraft had still not been given a Certificate of Airworthiness because, apart from many other problems, sizeable fatigue cracks had started to appear in her wings. This led to forecasts of an airframe life of only 5,000 hours. By 1952, £3.4 million had been spent on the development programme and BOAC, the only likely customer, had lost interest. It had instead opted for the Boeing Stratocruiser and the Lockheed Constellation, and ironically it operated them out of the third assembly hall at Filton while Heathrow Airport was being constructed.

In February 1952 the government took the decision to abandon the project and ordered that the only existing prototype, along with the half-completed fuselage of the second, should be broken up and sold for scrap. This took only 30 days and netted a paltry £10,000. All that is left today of the Brabazon is a nose wheel in London's Science Museum and a set of landing wheels and part of the fuselage in the new M Shed Museum. As a footnote, part of the Grange Infants' School at Tuffley, Gloucester, was recently discovered to be made from a fuselage section of the Brabazon. A spokesman for Save Britain's Heritage called it 'a charming example of the rapid rebuilding of Britain after World War Two'.

A complete white elephant? Yes and no. Commercially it had clearly been a total disaster. The Brabazon was in effect a flying time capsule, and even the normally very loyal *Bristol Evening Post* dubbed it the 'great Might-Have-Been'. On the other hand, the designers and engineers at Filton learned a tremendous amount from the project; and approximately half the money the government had come up with had gone into infrastructure like the runway extension and the enormous Brabazon assembly build-ing, occupying a total of eight acres, which was later used for Concorde. As far as the Bristol Aeroplane Company was concerned, all was definitely not lost. The people of Charlton begged to differ.

BRICKS

Made by The Cattybrook Brick Company

ISAMBARD KINGDOM BRUNEL was a man of huge energy with a finger in many engineering pies. In addition to designing the Clifton Suspension Bridge and the ss *Great Britain*, he was deeply involved with the development of the railways in England. In 1858 he appointed Charles Richardson as his resident engineer to supervise the building of a line linking Bristol with a ferry service using a paddle steamer to cross the Severn Estuary to South Wales. This Bristol and South Wales Union Railway involved building a lengthy tunnel near Patchway in north-west Bristol. When Richardson examined the red clay that was being excavated, he was impressed by its 'hardness and soundness' and quickly came to the conclusion that 'an article could be produced from this clay that was superior to any made in the neighbourhood and not excelled by any in the country'. Charles Richardson might have been prone to exaggeration but with an eye for the main chance, in 1860 he leased a few acres of land from the nearby Cattybrook farm and started building a small brick works which was completed in 1864.

Richardson's hunch paid off handsomely. In 1872 he was responsible for proposing a bill in Parliament 'to authorise the construction of the Severn Tunnel Railway'. It was duly passed, and work on the tunnel started the following year, with Charles Richardson its chief engineer. Needless to say, he did not have to look far for a supply of suitable bricks for this huge engineering project. Richardson's Cattybrook brickworks went on to supply 19.1 million of the 76.4 million bricks used to line the $4^1/_2$ mile-long (7,008m) tunnel, which was started in 1873 and finished in 1886. The Welsh, starting from the other side of the Severn, preferred to use their own bricks. Richardson made a fortune from wearing his two hats – engineer and brick maker, and even found time to invent the modern cricket bat, with its cane handle spliced into a willow blade.

Deep red Cattybrook bricks, made from clay calculated to be at least 400 million years old, were also used in the construction of many famous Bristol buildings. Several were in the Bristol Byzantine style, such as the Granary on Welsh Back and the Old Fish Market on Baldwin Street. On a bigger scale, Portishead power station, demolished in the late 1980s, Fry's chocolate factory at Keynsham and the Wills factories in Bedminster and Southville were also made from Cattybrook bricks. The bricks, which were particularly impervious to moisture and acids, also proved highly suitable in engineering work such as sewers, mines and bridges. At the turn of the century the company, under the chairmanship of Charles Richardson's son Frank, employed 250 men, women and children and made 20 million bricks a year. Two-thirds of this output went to South Wales (by rail through the Severn Tunnel!) and later all over the country and as far away as the West Indies.

Charles Richardson

THE
Cattybrook Brick Company
LIMITED.
Offices: 1 ST. STEPHEN'S CHAMBERS, BALDWIN STREET, BRISTOL.
Works: ALMONDSBURY, R.S.O., Glos.   *Station*: PATCHWAY, G.W.R.
Depôt: LAWRENCE HILL STATION, BRISTOL.
ERNEST E. STREET, Managing Director.

MANUFACTURERS OF
RED, WHITE AND BLUE FANCY BRICKS,
SPECIALLY MOULDED
Bricks for String Courses, Quoins, Arches, &c.
FIREBRICKS, BLUE AND BRINDLE VITRIFIED
BRICKS for STABLES, STREET PAVINGS, &c.
Also AGRICULTURAL DRAIN PIPES, &c., &c

Patchway Tunnel near Cattybrook farm

Cattybrook bricks were used in the Granary on Welsh Back

The modern Cattybrook brick works

In 1969 the Cattybrook Brick Company took over one of the few remaining Bristol brick firms at Shortwood, closed the brick works but used the clay until 2006. Nowadays the company is part of the Irish CRH group, and the site at Cattybrook employs 93 people. They still produce bricks on a huge scale – approximately 50 million a year, with an average of twelve million in stock at any time. The quarry from which the clay is extracted is now more than 100 feet deep in places and is far from exhausted, though often difficult to excavate because the strata are vertical as well as horizontal. Though millions of pounds were recently spent on new energy-efficient machinery at the brickworks, the gas-powered kilns, operating non-stop day and night, use as much fuel in a day as the average household does in three years. This is one large-scale Bristol manufacturing industry that is still going strong and is likely to continue to do so.

BRUSHES

Made by Kleeneze

THE KLEENEZE COMPANY was started by Harry Crook in 1928. He was born in Bristol in 1889 but his parents emigrated to the USA soon afterwards. In the States, Harry worked as a door-to-door salesman for the Fuller Brush Company, learning a lot about brushes and, more importantly, selling. He returned to Bristol in 1920 and, in 1923, he hired a small space under the stairs in a factory owned by his father-in-law in Chalks Road, Whitehall. There he started making brushes on a small work bench, using two vices for twisting the brush, a pair of pliers and scissors for trimming. Not content with making brushes, he also wanted to use the door-to-door techniques he had learned in the States on the residents of north Bristol. He was delighted to find they worked; between May and December 1923, sales amounted to £3,712. He could now afford to hire his first salesman and a year later sales had risen to £30,456. Harry Crook was well on his way to making a fortune.

Harry Crook, the founder of Kleeneze, when he became Lord Mayor of Bristol in 1955

By 1927 the business had expanded to such an extent that a purpose-designed factory was built in Hanham, with many of its workers being ex-soldiers from the First World War. By 1930 turnover topped £1 million. In the following decade the number of salesmen rose to 1,500 and it was reckoned that every household in the country received at least four visits a year from the Kleeneze man. Brushes for the domestic market alone used nearly 300 tons of fibres, bristles and wax, 865 trees, 150 tons of fine-gauge steel wire and 15 tons of horsehair.

The bristles for some brushes, collected from wild boars, were imported from China and in a 1950s booklet published by Kleeneze the extraordinary method of collection is described. 'A runway comprised of thorny hedges is constructed and the boars rounded up. All fences lead to an enclosure which has a number of exits fashioned to form long passages, through which the boars must force their way to escape. Thus a glorified "combing" is carried out during which many bristles are left behind in the hedges. They are collected and prepared in bundles of various lengths.'

In 1937 the Kleeneze salesmen started taking round tins of wax polish as well as brushes, and this marked the start of diversification. In 1950 Kleeneze described itself as 'Manufacturers of brushes (all types), mops, polishes and "Florigene" dust allayer' (whatever that long-forgotten product might be). Soon after that it advertised, among other things, Oatmeal Bath Cubes, which did not sell well. Chlorophyll toothpaste did better, as did Citrus Mist air freshener and stain removers, and the process of diversification continues today.

The basis of Kleeneze's success was always its direct selling method. In a typically

THE HOME OF Kleen-e-ze

"There's a bit of luck. You've saved me going out to get the wife a Christmas present."

American use of the language, Harry Crook dubbed his salesmen 'boosters'. They were called to regular sales meetings and made to sing morale-boosting songs from the Kleeneze song sheet, specially written by Harry's brother George. Boosters later became agents, and after 1982, agents became independent distributors; the man with the suitcase was replaced by a glossy catalogue delivered through the letter box, followed by a personal visit.

Kleeneze agents, then as now, worked entirely on commission – 21 per cent of everything they sold. Successful agents then became managers, who in turn recruited new agents and got a small percentage of everything they sold. Nowadays all Kleeneze distributors are self-employed, and they have to work hard; they distribute their catalogues, which cost them £1 each, and then re-walk the same route a few days later, knocking on doors and asking for them back or taking orders. They then log these orders on the Kleeneze website, receive the products and deliver them in return for cash payments. Finally, they take the money home, deduct their 21 per cent commission and send the rest to Kleeneze. It is not easy money. One former distributor said: 'It nearly broke our marriage. Stay away from Kleeneze. You will never earn any serious money.' Others are more positive. 'It is an ideal way to earn money around the kids and your life in general. I started this for my own pocket money, I worked hard and now I love it. The downsides? Well, it rains. Sometimes your books aren't put back

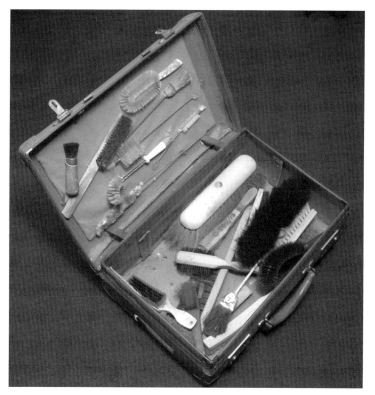

out. But for me Kleeneze has been proven. It does work.' Nowadays, the people at the top of the pyramid, according to the company's website, could take home as much as £500,000 a year.

Harry Crook himself went on to become a multi-millionaire, and in 1955 he was made Lord Mayor of Bristol. After becoming deaf he set up the Harry Crook Foundation at Bristol University which researches into the condition, and as a result he was granted an honorary degree in 1964. He died in 1970. In 1995 the company was taken over by Farepak Ltd and in May, 2004, after 75 years at its old address in Hanham, Kleeneze moved to new headquarters in Warmley, on the site of the old St Ivel factory. The company then became part of European Home Retail, which in 2006 was taken over by home shopping conglomerate Findell PLC, based in Accrington. Despite all these changes, the brand is still selling, in addition to brushes, more than 1,200 different household products, from talcum powder to toothpaste to fragranced toilet seat wipes to a doormat with the welcoming message 'Oh no, not you again!' Its connection with Bristol is almost severed, but it is certainly not forgotten.

9 BUSES

Made by Bristol Commercial Vehicles

FIRST CAME TRAMS, more specifically the Bristol Tramways and Carriage Company, and then came buses. Their job was to pick up passengers from the more outlying or hilly parts of Bristol and take them to the nearest convenient tram stop. Interestingly, the posh residents of Clifton did not really approve of trams, perhaps because they were too modern, but preferred horse buses because they looked more like traditional open carriages.

Motor buses first appeared on the streets of Bristol in 1906, on the route to Clifton. Less than two years later, Sir George White and his company decided they could build better buses than the ones they were buying and in 1908 started hand-building the vehicles one at a time at the Brislington tram depot. By this time Sir George had his fingers in three different forms of transport – aircraft, trams and buses – and all shared the same familiar Bristol scroll insignia. In 1912 bus production was moved to a new factory in Bath Road, Brislington, which was given the decidedly unevocative name of Motor Constructional Works, or MCW for short.

In the 1920s the company expanded rapidly, and Bristol buses were sold to operators as far afield as Cornwall, Sunderland and Manchester. During the Second World War the works switched to making planes and specialist vehicles such as searchlight trailers, reverting to producing single and double-decker buses when peace returned. Many were exported to big Commonwealth markets such as India and South Africa.

In 1953, after lengthy development work that had started in 1949, the company started making one of its most famous buses, the Lodekka, a 73-seat double-decker with a revolutionary design. The main problem with double-deckers is their height. Up until that time they had been between 14 and 15 feet high, which meant that routes were often limited by low bridges. The engineers at Bristol came up with an ingenious solution, locating the propeller shaft to one side of the bus, under the seats, instead of down the middle. It meant the floor downstairs could be flat and considerably lower, resulting in the overall height of the bus being reduced to 13 feet 6 inches. This gave the Lodekka a considerable advantage over its competitors. Built in Brislington between 1953 and 1968 it was extremely successful, with more than 5,200 produced. They were sold to operators as far afield as West Yorkshire, Brighton, the Eastern counties and Scotland, painted in liveries varying from red to green to blue to cream.

The historic but informal connection with Sir George White's aircraft company at Filton continued to the extent that the latter did the bus company a favour by testing its chassis to destruction on its test rigs. An odd feature of the construction of the Bristol buses at one time was the fact that when half-finished they had to be driven

A restored Bristol Lodekka driving out of Millennium Square

The bare chassis of three Lodekkas ready to be driven to Lowestoft for bodies and seats to be fitted

265 miles (before the coming of motorways) in bare chassis form to the Eastern Coachworks at Lowestoft for their bodies and seats to be fitted. The journey took two days and involved drivers dressing up as warmly as possible in Second World War bomber crew sheepskin jackets and helmets, crouching down behind a plywood wind-screen for the slow and freezing-cold journey.

On October 1, 1965, the Leyland Motor Corporation acquired a 25 per cent interest in Bristol Commercial Vehicles and then, at the end of 1982, complete control of the company. For reasons best known to themselves, they closed the works less than a year later, although at the time they had a full order book. They moved production of buses to factories in Lancashire and Cumbria and finally, when taken over by Volvo,

Bristol Commercial Vehicles Limited
Bath Road,
Brislington,
Bristol 4.
Telephone Bristol 77613

BRISTOL

above: another well-preserved Bristol Lodekka

right: a Bristol VR on display at the Earls Court Motor Show in 1966

to Scotland. Capitalism can sometimes work in mysterious ways.

Today the Bristol bus factory in Brislington is a trading estate. For a time, Lodekkas were relegated to driver-training duties before finally being pensioned off. They had, however, a last brief moment of glory when they appeared in the popular 1970s sitcom *On the Buses*, with Reg Varney as a plausible driver but unlikely part-time Lothario, but to many bus-loving viewers, the Lodekka, operated at the time by Eastern National in Essex, was the real star of the show, which ran to 74 episodes and three spin-off films. Lodekkas were built to last and there are still plenty of them on the road today, some used as play buses for children, others on open-top tourist routes in places like Bath. Many have even ended up on the other side of the Atlantic where, painted red and with Trafalgar Square or Piccadilly Circus inserted into their destination boxes, they masquerade as genuine London buses although in real life, London Transport never bought a single Lodekka.

CARAVANS

Made by Bailey Caravans

MARTIN BAILEY WAS THE MAN who started Bailey Caravans. He worked at the Bristol Aeroplane Company in Filton as a sheet metal worker during the Second World War. When peace reurned and aircraft production was cut back, he turned to cabinet making and helped to produce the then ubiquitous 'Utility' furniture. In 1947 he was approached by a friend who wanted to buy some plywood, which was strictly rationed. He said he wanted to build a caravan, and this gave Martin Bailey the idea. He sketched a design that looked a bit like a wardrobe on wheels, and for the next six months he worked on it in his spare time in his garage at home in Ashton Gate. Eventually the first Bailey caravan was complete, and in 1948 he sold it at an auction at Ashton Gate market for £200.

Martin Bailey then moved into a small workshop – originally the old school house on Bedminster Down – and started making caravans for a living. In November 1948 the first quirky advertisement for a Bailey caravan appeared: 'The Saint adds another string to his harp, the Bailey Minor. Full headroom, customers over 7 feet tall supplied with aspirin tablets. Really waterproof – if it leaks we'll shoot the makers. Springs in every bed – one for Ma, one for Dad and two in reserve. Everything for £495 including insulation, jockey wheel, wine cellar and kettle.' The Minor was followed in 1955 by the Maestro, which was high-tech at the time. It had an all-aluminium exterior, except for its canvas roof, a four-ring gas cooker, gas lighting and the most advanced feature of all, a chemical toilet. All this for only £288!

Bailey's business grew steadily until, after 12 years, it was running out of space. In 1960 it moved to an extensive site in South Liberty Lane, Ashton Vale, which in the nineteenth century was a brickworks surrounded by coal mines, and much later served as a dumping ground for trams damaged beyond repair during the 1940 Blitz on Bristol. This expansion came just at the right time because car ownership during the 1960s was booming. In 1977 Martin Bailey retired and his business was bought by the Howard family and became Bailey Caravans Ltd. Today the company is still owned by the same family and has continued to expand. It now has a one-third share of the British market, with a turnover in 2009 of £87.5 million. Around 350 people work for Bailey's, and together they make about 40 caravans a day, and more than 8,500 a year. On the fully automated production line, one caravan takes less than three hours to build. It is still very much a south Bristol firm and reckons that 85 per cent of its workforce live within five minutes' drive of the factory.

Owners of Bailey caravans are very loyal to the brand. There is even a 500-member Bailey Caravan Club, its most famous member probably being the former Foreign

One of Martin Bailey's very first caravans, the Maestro, built in 1955

The production line at the Bailey factory in Ashton Vale

The top-of-the range Unicorn Valencia

Secretary Margaret Beckett. She and her husband regularly took their Pageant Champagne on holiday to France, with a posse of Secret Service personnel following on behind.

In marked contrast with Martin Bailey's first caravan, today's top-of-the-range Bailey Unicorn Valencia costs £18,490 and comes with a state-of-the-art home entertainment system featuring a radio/CD/MP3/DVD and the latest flat-screen digital TV, full central heating, a heated towel rail and an eye-level stainless steel microwave. No wonder the sales brochure prefers to describe it as a 'touring home' rather than a mere caravan. In fact it is more like a large studio flat on wheels, except that it can comfortably sleep six people.

11 CARS

Made by Bristol Car Company

MOST PEOPLE ASSUME that Bristol cars have always been quintessentially British, and nowadays they are. But their origins, at least, can be traced back to pre-war Germany. The Bristol Car Company was set up just after the Second World War when the Bristol Aeroplane Company had very few orders for aircraft but a surplus of highly skilled workers. Twelve years before that, in 1934, a car enthusiast and businessman named H J Aldington had negotiated with the head of BMW, Franz Josef Popp, the right to import and sell BMWs in Britain under the name Frazer Nash BMW. Then came the war, and the BMW works in Germany were almost totally destroyed by Allied bombing.

Popp was imprisoned by the Americans for his alleged Nazi sympathies; but Aldington, who was still in the army, used his high-up military contacts to visit Popp in jail and also to obtain permission to visit the bombed-out BMW works. At the time they were in the newly designated United States zone of occupation and the Americans were planning to dismantle the surviving parts of the production lines and ship them back home. According to company legend, Aldington and two engineers from Bristol visited the factory just in time. They said they were there to study high-altitude aircraft testing equipment but in reality were intent on searching the design office for anything connected with BMW's pre-war cars. Their search was not in vain, and they managed to 'liberate' the blueprints and technical drawings of the BMW sports cars, along with two engines. These they then crated and exported back to Bristol in a Stirling bomber as 'war reparations'.

Dr Fritz Fielder, who had been BMW's chief engine designer and had spent some time in prison (along with Dr Ferdinand Porsche), was then recruited to help design the first Bristol car, the 400. It came out in September 1946 and bore an uncanny, although perhaps to be expected, resemblance to the pre-war BMW 327. It even carried the familiar BMW double-kidney radiator grille, albeit with a newly designed Bristol badge on the bonnet. Under the skin, however, the engine had been modified and converted from metric to Imperial and generally made more robust. The car cost a jaw-dropping £2,373 14s 6d.

In 1947 the Aldington team and Bristol Cars parted company, and soon after that came the first 'real' Bristol, the radically new 401. It is arguably the most beautiful car Bristol has ever produced. Its engine was still the tried and tested BMW 2 litre, upgraded with a few more minor modifications. By this time it produced 85 bhp, which was enough to propel it to 60 mph in 16 seconds and then on to a top speed of 97 mph, though most owners were understandably convinced it was capable of 100. By modern standards, of course, this is glacially slow – a Ford Fiesta diesel is faster –

but in the late 1940s it was sensational for a luxury car capable of carrying five people at a pinch. It was the striking, aerodynamic, all-aluminium bodywork that really marked out the 401, however. Beautifully curved panels covered a tubular steel framework and, perhaps because aircraft engineers had helped test it in the Bristol Aeroplane Company's wind tunnel, it had no door handles but large, recessed push buttons, aircraft door locks and recessed bumpers. The car cost £3,532 12s 3d, which would have bought you three Jaguar XK120s or eight Ford Populars, and even at that price you had to pay an extra £55 4s 6d for a radio and £35 for a heater. After that, the co-operation between aircraft and car designers at Filton continued; the air intake on the Bristol 404, for example, was an exact scaled-down version of the Brabazon's!

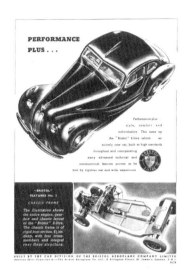

Bristol and BMW, of course, have gone their very separate ways. BMW now produces more than a million cars a year and in March 2011, when Bristol went into administration, the company was building around 150 cars a year, though the exact figure was a closely guarded secret. In April, Bristol was bought by Frazer-Nash, re-establishing a link that went back 65 years to the beginnings of Bristol Cars in the 1940s. Although it is unlikely that any more cars will be built at Filton, the Bristol name may live on as 'the only luxury car manufacturer that remains in private British hands' with vehicles 'coach built by proud and conscientious artisans'.

Driving a Bristol car in Bristol is an experience in itself. Ex-Bristol Aeroplane Company employees are likely to accost you as soon as you get out of it and reminisce about how they used to polish gearbox components, press aluminium panels or cut leather trim for Bristol cars, having been sent over from the aircraft factory's night shift when it was quiet. It really was true that Bristol cars were made, in part at least, by the same engineers and craftsmen that made the Britannia and Concorde. Others look back nostalgically to the time when allegedly every Bristol was tested by the managing director himself on the main Filton runway, to make sure it really could do 100 mph. Bristol aficionados include two Conservative ex-Cabinet ministers, John Patten and William Waldegrave. Patten once wrote: 'With Bristols, discretion is the over-riding virtue. Name plates are so small they can hardly be seen.' Waldegrave commented: 'It was always my ambition as a boy to own a Bristol, and I managed to buy one for £600 in 1973. My 402 is my pride and joy. I would never sell it.' Other less predictable owners are said to include, or have included, Noel Gallagher, Tina Turner, Bono, Jimmy Carter and Peter Sellers, who bought more than 60 of them. According to Tony Crook, ex-RAF fighter pilot and a former owner of Bristol Cars: 'Eventually we had a Sellers' service bay, with two full-time mechanics working purely on his cars.' Bristol fans also remember the classic line delivered by wheeler-dealer Boysie in *Only Fools and Horses*: 'I'm going to Bristol to see a man about a Capri. I wish it was the other way round.'

By the end of the 1950s, two litres was no longer enough for a high-performance

A Bristol 403 with its owner, Chief Test
Pilot Bill Pegg parked next to the
Brabazon (see page 23)

A Bristol 404 (left) and a 405 at Filton

car. All Bristols since then have been powered by huge American engines, some of them turbo-charged, to provide 'adequate' horsepower, a piece of typically British understatement. Despite their massive power, Tony Crook once remarked: 'A Bristol is a very safe car. We've only lost three owners in 60 years, and one of those deliberately drove off a precipice!'

The owner at administration, Toby Silverton, made his fortune in aircraft spare parts. He was content for Bristol Cars to stay small, employing about 100 people and producing a more or less steady 150 cars a year with a waiting list of between a year and 18 months. Bristol's current top-of-the-range car, the Fighter T (denoting twin-turbo), has an eight-litre V10 engine producing a mind-boggling 1012 b.h.p., a theoretical top speed of 270 mph (although it is normally limited to 'a more than adequate' 225 mph) and acceleration from 0-60 m.p.h. in less than 3.5 seconds. It costs a staggering £346,625, but for that price a radio and heater are included these days. The only place you can buy one is from the company's showroom on Kensington High Street – a fitting address for 'Great Britain's most exclusive Luxury Car'.

The Bristol Fighter

CASUALTY

Made by the BBC

The ever-present Charlie Fairhead, played by Derek Thompson

THERE WAS A TIME IN THE 1960s when ITV's *Emergency Ward 10* dominated the ratings. When that particular medical soap no longer quickened the nation's pulse and was axed it was assumed that the hospital drama had had its day. But then a young BBC script editor, Jeremy Brock, who had studied at Bristol University, ended up in the Bristol Royal Infirmary casualty department after an accident. While waiting to be treated he got into conversation with a charge nurse, Peter Salt, and this chance encounter gave him the idea for a series of programmes based on the working lives of staff in an inner-city casualty department. Jeremy was working on the cop show *Juliet Bravo* at the time, but with his colleague Paul Unwin he put together a one-page treatment for a new show which was a fresh, new approach to the hospital drama genre. The BBC was relying on *Juliet Bravo* to keep up its ratings on Saturday evenings, and to replace it, it had to choose between a safe option – a cosy drama series based on a cottage hospital – and Brock and Unwin's provisionally named *Front Line*, later changed to *Casualty*. 'I went for *Casualty*,' the Head of Drama explained, 'because there was a feeling of life and passion to it, and I was anxious for new, young people to create something.' A series of 15 programmes was commissioned and the first episode, Gas, hit the nation's screens on September 8, 1986.

The opening sequence showed a very young looking charge nurse called Charlie Fairhead, played by Derek Thompson, driving to work across the Clifton Suspension Bridge in a battered yellow VW Beetle and stubbing out a cigarette as he got out of his car. There were ten main staff members at that time, including Nurse Duffy and a staff nurse, Clive King, who suffered and put up with sporadic racial taunts from patients because he was black. In other words, it was a doctors and nurses show that tried hard for realism. That charge nurse at the BRI, Peter Salt, went on to become a medical adviser to the series, a role which 24 years later he still fills. Jeremy Brock later commented: 'What we stumbled on was a formula that is pretty cast-iron. When those hospital doors bang open, the drama begins.'

From the start, *Casualty* deliberately avoided the sentimentalism that besets most American hospital shows. A study in the *British Medical Journal* illustrated the point. Cardiac arrests occur frequently in hospital A&E dramas – they are clichés, but as cliff-hangers they work. In *Casualty* the number of patients who survive – one in four – exactly reflects the percentage who survive in real life. In the equivalent American *ER*, three-quarters 'make it'; that is American optimism, but it is not realism.

When it started, *Casualty* came in for a huge amount of criticism. Mrs Thatcher's government objected because it overtly campaigned against funding cuts in the NHS,

The deliberately anonymous-looking building in St Philips, the home of *Casualty* until summer 2011

and the Royal College of Nursing criticised the less-than-flattering way nurses were sometimes portrayed. There was talk of the show being axed, but by this time ratings had started to climb and a second series was already half-completed. Most of them were made in a warehouse on an industrial estate in St Philips equipped and furnished to make it look like a fully-operational casualty ward. The decision was made to carry on regardless.

A past producer of *Casualty* summed up the programme's ethos:

> The audience wants to see our characters as doctors and nurses, and we also believe very strongly that it is the realism of it that makes the show sustainable. If we didn't make it real, it would become melodrama very quickly.

There was a telling example of life imitating art in the second series. Viewers had just finished watching an episode in which dead and dying people were being pulled from the wreckage of a house bombed by the IRA when, hours later, there came news of the Enniskillen bombing.

Emergencies at the heart of each episode have included murders, muggings, stabbings, fires, drownings, poisonings, explosions, collisions and crashes. The script writers clearly have a hard job dreaming up new variations on this litany of woes, but when it comes to sub-plots the writers have more freedom and the show is never formulaic. It remains a clever mix of ongoing story lines based on the central characters and stand-alone mini-dramas. Even today it is still a quality show and not just a tired hospital soap – producers point to a recent BAFTA award – and researchers and writers make regular visits to the BRI A&E department, shadowing doctors and nurses and learning a lot about the realities of the place, blood, vomit and all.

Casualty's prime time ratings success – in 1994 it peaked at 17.2 million viewers an episode – led in 1999 to an equally popular spin-off, *Holby City*, set in the same hospital's surgical ward, which goes out on Tuesday evenings. *Casualty* has inevitably come down off that 1994 peak, with more recent viewing figures of seven or eight million; by today's multi-channel standards that is still very impressive, although it must help that the show has a 50-minute prime time slot on a Saturday evening. What is incredible is the number of episodes made and shown – 48 a year. This relentless pace means that there are always two episodes being shot at the same time, each taking

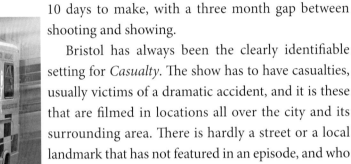

10 days to make, with a three month gap between shooting and showing.

Bristol has always been the clearly identifiable setting for *Casualty*. The show has to have casualties, usually victims of a dramatic accident, and it is these that are filmed in locations all over the city and its surrounding area. There is hardly a street or a local landmark that has not featured in an episode, and who has not noticed at some time those small fluorescent arrows with cryptic letters tied to lamp posts, telling the location crew where exactly to go?

Working as an actor on a television soap, or 'continuing drama', as they prefer to call it, can be a precarious way of earning a living. A character might be deemed expendable if, in the short term at least, their dramatic exit will bump up the ratings. In August 2011 the show moved to Wales. In the long run, will it mean more jobs for Welsh actors? Will the show lose its strong identity as a result of the move?

Casualty is still pulling in the viewers more than 20 years after it first started, and for 48 weeks of the year it remains at the heart of the BBC ratings war on a Saturday night. It is just regrettable that it's no longer made in Bristol. Saturday evenings will never be quite the same again.

CELESTINE

13

Mined by the Bristol Mineral and Land Company

NOT A LOT OF PEOPLE HAVE HEARD OF CELESTINE, and even fewer know that at one time it was one of the Bristol area's most valuable products. It might sound like a girl's name but in fact it is the principal commercial source of strontium sulphate or spar. It was called celestine, from the Latin caelestialis, meaning 'heavenly', because of the pale blue colour it sometimes has. The history of celestine goes back 220 million years to the Triassic period, when the Bristol area and most of Britain was comparable to today's Sahara Desert, with lagoons lapping round its edges. The water eventually evaporated, deposits of celestine were left, and over the next 28 million years they were buried under much harder rocks. These were gradually eroded until, very recently in the history of the world, celestine was again found near the surface.

Celestine workings near Yate

Deposits of this strange mineral are extremely rare, so rare that the north Bristol area, between Yate and Wickwar, at one time produced more than 90 per cent of the world's output. It was first excavated on a small scale in about 1875, but in 1890 a German sugar refining company sent scouts to the Bristol area and employed local labour to dig small pits and bore for it. When sizeable deposits had been found they employed farm workers to load it onto horse-drawn carts which in turn took it to the nearest railway station and thence to Avonmouth for shipping to Germany. There it was used in a new sugar-beet refining process. Production increased so much that in 1912 the Bristol Mineral and Land Company was formed.

Of course trade with Germany was abruptly halted by the First World War, but other uses for celestine were found by the British army. Because it produces a brilliant crimson flame it was used in signal flares, tracer bullets and rockets, and the company continued to do well. Eventually, in 1941, when it was still the only producer in Britain, it was taken over by Albright and Wilson, who in 1969 sold it to the English China Clay Company. From 1945 until 1989, during the Cold War, celestine was one of a number of products banned from being exported to countries behind the Iron Curtain. Demand boomed again during the Vietnam war, when more than two-thirds of the production of celestine, about 7,000 tons a year, was exported to the USA. Happily, it also had some decidedly non-military uses, including the production of

78 rpm gramophone records and hair remover creams.

In addition to the Yate area celestine was mined just south of the river Avon, around Abbots Leigh. Sir Henry Miles, squire of Leigh Court, gave permission to an enterprising local man called R B Withers of Pill to prospect for minerals on the estate, and on finding sizeable deposits of celestine he dug pits up to 20 feet deep to extract it by pick and shovel. He then utilised the tramway through the quaintly named Paradise Bottom valley to the small Miles Dock, facilities that had been built to handle the stone for building Leigh Court, which was completed in 1814. The mining of celestine there ceased in 1912, long before R B Withers might have discovered that his product could be put to good use in removing hair from ladies' legs.

Most celestine workings in the Bristol area closed down in the 1960s but one, at Hall End Farm, kept going until 1994. Yate Shopping Centre is built over what was earlier a celestine quarry, and celestine pits later formed the lakes in Kingsgate Park which are now home to a number of great crested newts. Today, however, there is hardly a trace of what was once one of Bristol's most profitable industries.

CHOLCOLATES

14

Made by Guilbert's

IN CASE YOU HAVEN'T HEARD OF IT, Guilbert's is a small Bristol firm making very special hand-made chocolates. The chocolates are made and sold from their own shop in one of the oldest streets in Bristol where, appropriately enough, Joseph Fry first started his chocolate business over 250 years ago (see the story of Turkish Delight later in this book). Guilbert's shop and factory, at 16 and 17 Small Street, is in a building which dates from the early fifteenth century and is believed to be the oldest building in Bristol still in commercial use.

Inside Guilbert's shop in Small Street

The company was started by a young Swiss-Belgian called Piers Guilbert (Piers was an anglicisation of Pearce) who came to Bristol in the early 1900s. He fell in love with a Bristol girl, Olive May, decided to marry her and stay in Bristol. Coming from Belgium he knew a bit about chocolates so in 1910 he started making chocolates to his own recipe in a small factory behind a shop at 40, Park Street. Guilbert sold the business 15 years later but the company deliberately kept his name perhaps because, when it comes to selling products like hand-made chocolates, a foreign-sounding name never did any harm. It remained in Park Street until badly damaged by bombing during the Second World War. It changed hands again and then in 1958 moved to Leonard Lane, just off Corn Street, where it was subsequently managed and then owned by Alan and Wendy White. Alan had joined the company in 1980 as an apprentice chocolatier straight after leaving school in Hartcliffe. At work he met Wendy Baugh who had recently joined the firm as a dipper. They married and had six children, four of whom have worked for the firm at various times, not forgetting Alan's mother – making it three generations altogether. The Whites clearly believe in keeping it in the family.

In 2009 Alan was contacted by an American businessman, Roger Buoy. Roger was born and raised in Southmead, Bristol but left Britain in the 1960s to work in the USA. He stayed there for over 40 years and has a mid-Atlantic accent to prove it. He became a very successful businessman, with companies in South Africa, Australia and Portugal as well as in the USA. Now living some of the time in north Somerset, where he has a design studio, he continues to fly all over the world, managing his numerous businesses. Roger tells the story in his own words:

> My wife and I were having a look around a little gift shop in Thornbury, because we're always searching for Bristolian products to send back to our family in the States. I spotted a box of Guilbert's chocolates, and despite having been brought up here, I have to confess I'd never heard of them. When I bit into that Guilbert's chocolate I realised it was the best rose and violet cream I had ever tasted. I was

so impressed I actually telephoned Guilbert's and spoke to Alan White. I said, you have a tremendous product and a couple of weeks later we started talking business.

Roger brought his expertise in marketing and packaging design to Guilbert's and the brand was relaunched in September 2009. Centenary tins were introduced each one showing a different view of Bristol's favourite landmarks. Customers now include Harvey Nichols, Fortnum & Mason in London, the Bristol Guild on Park Street and the Duty Free at Bristol Airport as well as many more high-end retailers. Guilbert's continues to roll out its new look including advertisements throughout the Bristol City ground at Ashton Gate – the away end has even been officially renamed the Guilbert's Wedlock Stand. Guilbert's is very proud of its Bristol roots!

Meanwhile the husband-and-wife team of Alan and Wendy White continue to do the chocolate-making in Small Street, creating 'the finest, hand-dipped, overtly indulgent chocolates and confections'. Guilbert's work with the finest Belgian couverture (a very high quality chocolate that contains extra cocoa butter) which is a link back to Guilbert's origins. It's delivered about once a fortnight in big 25-kilo boxes. In one year they use about 12 tons of plain, milk and white chocolate which is then blended and filled to Guilbert's own very traditional recipes.

The company employs eight people, most of them women, to make the individual chocolates. Men, according to Alan White, aren't usually as good as women except for heavier jobs. Learning to be a chocolate maker takes from three to six months and once trained, one skilled dipper can make as many as 100lbs of individual chocolates a day. Occasionally Guilbert's will have a job vacancy which they advertise in newsagents' windows on the Gloucester Road. The pay is nothing special but the promise of free chocolates usually brings plenty of job applicants.

Production methods haven't changed much in nearly a century – one of the tricks of the trade is to gently warm and then keep the chocolate at a constant temperature all day using two light bulbs to keep it just soft enough to work with. They have modernised to some extent though: they now use an electric mixer rather than mixing by hand. Centres or fillings include walnut and brazil caramels, coffee truffles and, most popular of all, rose and violet creams –the sort of chocolates that Miss Marple might have gorged herself on while solving one of her many murder mysteries. Most of the finished chocolates are then packed into boxes one by one – nothing is very mechanised at Guilbert's.

You can buy Guilbert's chocolates direct from their shop in Small Street (almost opposite the Law Courts). There you can also choose your own combination of loose chocolates with whatever fillings you like, all put carefully into a special box, and then tied up with a special Guilbert's ribbon. It's worth buying direct from the factory just for the smell of chocolate which hits you as soon as you open the door.

The hand-made chocolates and the traditional way they're made may be old-fashioned in many ways but the firm has now definitely moved into the twenty-first century. As Roger Buoy put it: 'Guilbert's chocolates have been a part of Bristol's story for the last century, and I think they are going to be around for a good many years to come.'

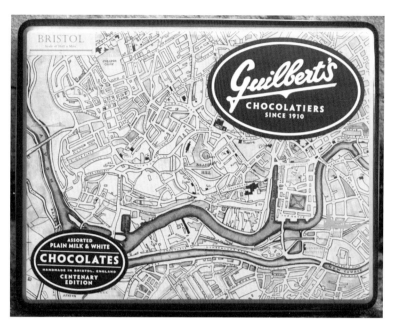

A centenary tin

15   CIDER

Made by Coates

Redvers Coate

DURING THE NINETEENTH CENTURY, cider made in Somerset and around Bristol was for the most part rough scrumpy. It was cloudy, it tasted of rotten apples and a few other things besides but it was strong and cheap. Many men with blue noses and red-veined cheeks used to sit in local pubs drinking nothing else. But then in 1887, the government passed a law forbidding farmers to pay their workers in the form of several pints, or in some cases gallons, of strong cider. As a result, cider drinking was in decline at the start of the twentieth century. But in 1921, Redvers Coate, the son of a hay merchant from Bridgwater who had just got a degree in chemistry from Bristol University, was invited to lunch by his girlfriend's clergyman father. To Redvers's surprise this vicar insisted on drinking a considerable quantity of cider with his lunch and then offered him this advice:

> You're an educated fellow, young Redvers, but as far as I can see you have no job
> to go to. Why don't you start a company to make this fine drink that you and I
> are sharing?

Redvers Coate subsequently married Mary Catlow, the vicar's daughter, and took his father-in-law's advice. With the help of Professor Bertie Barker he got an unpaid job for a year at the Long Ashton Research Station which was later responsible for 'inventing' Ribena (see page 127). That now defunct research station was called, when it was founded in 1903, the National Fruit and Cider Institute, and it spent a considerable time researching into the best cider apple varieties and the optimum growing conditions for them. Redvers Coate learned a lot in a relatively short time and came to the conclusion that the apple orchards of Somerset could produce better quality cider than traditional cheap scrumpy. If Herefordshire could make a profitable industry out of its apples, why not Somerset? So, at the age of just 23, with the help of money borrowed from family and friends, he opened a small cider works in a shed which was once an old saw mill on Nailsea High Street. He had, he wrote later, 'the ridiculous idea that I would like to build up and run the biggest cider-making business in the country.' Most of the money was spent on three glass-lined vats each containing 10,000 gallons.

To begin with the factory employed six people, including Coate himself. After only a year Coates won the first three prizes in a national cider-making competition. He was a happy man. But not for long. As he remarked later:

> I thought the important thing was just to make good cider, really good cider,

and I never thought about the selling part of it. So we had all this beautiful cider
and nobody knew about it, nobody wanted to buy it.

That's when the hard work really started – selling his prize-winning cider in the face
of fierce competition from established cider-makers like Bulmers and Whiteways. 'I
was out every night, calling on the pubs that weren't tied,' Redvers said. 'I found this
necessary pub-crawling very hard work. I felt as if I was a commercial traveller in
search of sales.'

His next job was to persuade enough local farmers to supply him with the apples
he needed. When demand increased before and during the war he had to accept
anything he could get. But quality wasn't sacrificed for quantity. Every day at 12.30
pm, Coate organised a tasting session to check that the cider was as good, if not better,
than the previous year's vintage.

By the time the Second World War started Coates Cider employed up to 125 people.
Most of these men went off to fight leaving only older men and women to carry on. They
were eventually joined by boys and young men evacuated from London and then Italian
prisoners of war from a POW camp at Ashton Court just outside Bristol. The prisoners
arrived every day in a coach, without any guards, and reputedly got on very well with
the locals. Redvers Coate himself worked as an Army Welfare Officer, dealing with the
domestic problems of men away fighting, and also Head Air Raid Warden for the Wraxall area when Bristol was suffering repeated heavy bombing raids.

Like many local businesses, Coates cider did very well in the war years, helped by

A specially-built tanker being filled with Coates cider in the early 1960s

Coates comes up from Somerset

the fact that beer was in short supply. Many people, including American servicemen over here preparing for D-Day, acquired a taste for cider. After the war, when beer rationing came to an end, Coate decided not to compete head-on with beer. 'I came to the conclusion that bottled cider was a thing of the future and so it proved. To me cider was something to be sold in the off-licence and shops rather than pubs.' He then had to persuade Somerset farmers to grow for him new varieties of apple tree with names like Slack Ma Girdle, Sweet Alford, Kingston Black, Hangdown, Yarlington Mill and Sheep's Nose. He succeeded and Coates Cider became so successful that in 1956 Showerings of Shepton Mallet, the makers of that now distinctly unfashionable drink Babycham, made Coate an offer he couldn't refuse. The two companies merged and cider production was moved to a big new 13-acre site. Redvers Coate commented, 'We shall now see to it that good advertising and marketing support is used for Somerset cider which is one of the world's most natural and healthy drinks.'

By the 1960s production and the number of people working for Coates Cider had doubled and the company proudly announced that its products were exported to over 30 countries, including Columbia, Egypt, Sudan, India and Mauritius. By this time over a thousand Somerset farmers were supplying Coates with cider apples and over 200 tons of apples a day were being processed, extracting 180 gallons of juice from each ton of apples. This success was helped by the infuriatingly memorable television advertising campaign featuring a group of cartoon yokels singing, 'Coates comz up from Zumerzet where the zider apples grow, There's nothing like Coates zider, To make a party go'.

Redvers Coate became semi-retired in 1966 after 41 years as managing director and following the advice of his cider-drinking father-in-law. According to his son Peter he was a man with a real passion for cider-making who also found time to watch Somerset play cricket and Bristol play rugby and also mess about in a small boat which he kept down on the Beaulieu River in Hampshire. He retained his lifelong interest in apples and cider, so much so that his house in Abbots Leigh had a 24-acre experimental apple orchard in which he walked every day with his two corgies, constantly tending, grafting and replanting. He also carried on drinking cider all his life, preferring Coates Festival Vat which was specially brewed to commemorate the Festival of Britain in 1951. Peter, whom he encouraged to drink cider from the age of eight, went on to become a much-respected local artist although his father, not surprisingly, hoped that he would also become a cider maker and take over the business.

After the merger with Showerings, production of Coates cider was eventually moved to Shepton Mallet and in 1974 the Nailsea cider factory was finally closed with the loss of 250 jobs. 110 huge oak vats, most with a capacity of 50,000 gallons and with names like Spitfire and Churchill, Roosevelt and Stalin, Caesar and Cleopatra (the vats had originally been bought from Guinness in London and George's the brewers in Bristol), had to be sold. The Coates Cider name finally disappeared in 1994. There's now an office block on the site called Coates House but that's the only reminder of what was once a thriving local industry.

Redvers Coate died in 1985 at Abbots Leigh, aged 84, two days after celebrating his diamond wedding anniversary to Mary, the vicar's daughter. He was a man who always had his priorities right and never forgot that the most valuable asset of any business is the people working in it. At his funeral in Wraxall church it was said, 'He was an extremely tough and tenacious person, yet the kindest and most gentle of men.' He, perhaps more than anyone else, firmly believed that 'cider is to Englishmen what wine is to Frenchmen' and created from nothing an important new local industry to prove it.

Redvers Coate at his 'experimental cider orchard' in Abbots Leigh

16 CIGARETTES

Made by W D & H O Wills

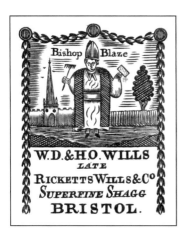

THE STORY OF HOW HENRY OVERTON WILLS came from Salisbury and in 1787 became a partner in a small tobacconist's business in Castle Street has been told many times. The Wills business for its first 75 years or so was based on pipe tobacco with wonderfully evocative names such as Bishops Blaze, Superfine Shag, Bogie Roll, Bright Red Rag and Shag Birds Eye. Then things started to change. W D Wills died in 1865 and his brother H O Wills junior in 1871 – ironically, both were non-smokers – and the company came under the control of William Henry Wills. He spotted the new trend in the tobacco industry, the growing popularity of cigarettes, which had started in the Crimean War when British troops caught the habit from their French and Turkish allies. It was cigarettes that were to become the basis of Wills' spectacular growth in the second half of the nineteenth century, although it was not until 1871 that it marketed its first brand, the Bristol. This soon became their most popular brand although ironically, it was made at the company's London factory.

In 1878 electric light was installed in the Wills factory in Redcliff Street, which made it so ahead of its time that the Crown Prince of Siam made a special trip to Bristol to marvel at this amazing new piece of technology. In other respects, however, this was a traditional factory, and it did not find switching from pipe tobacco to cigarette making easy. The idea of wrapping tobacco in a paper tube was so radically different that the Wills workers had to be specially trained by a Russian foreman and expert cigarette maker with the unlikely-sounding name of Bogosoff.

In 1874, with a clever piece of marketing, Wills went for the top end of the market with its famous Passing Cloud brand; its unique oval shape and delicate pink hue made it the sort of cigarette Oscar Wilde would almost certainly have smoked. Three Castles followed four years later, a touch more manly, with the packet showing a moored sailing ship, three casks of tobacco on the quay and a young man from the eighteenth century reclining and enjoying a Wills cigarette; it identified the Wills' brand for the next 70 years.

It was in 1883 that Wills got into the mass market seriously when H H (Harry) Wills, second son of H O Wills the third, started working for the family firm full-time. In that year he installed a wooden Bonsack cigarette-making machine in the factory in Redcliff Street, some three years after the American James Albert Bonsack had first patented it. The senior partners in the firm were relative Luddites, and were also concerned that the machine would throw many Wills girls out of work, but Harry said he was prepared to leave if it was not a success. Wills had to pay Bonsack a royalty on every cigarette made, but the machine more than paid for itself and Harry Wills soon installed another, this time an iron model. In 1884 Wills' cigarette production was

The Wills shop at 112 Redcliff Street, after merging with Peter Lilley in 1791

BRISTOL AND TOBACCO
W. D. & H. O. WILLS
Branch of the Imperial Tobacco Co. (of Great Britain and Ireland), Ltd.

Mr. H. O. WILLS, 1761-1826

Mr. W. D. WILLS, 1797-1865

Mr. H. O. WILLS, 1800-1871

HO 1761-1826, WD 1797-1865 and HO 1800-1871

some six million, the next year around nine million and by 1886 it had risen to 14 million. By 1901 Wills had 22 Bonsack machines working flat-out, and in 1904 uprated versions were each producing 600 cigarettes a minute.

Production costs were of course slashed, but the real breakthrough for Wills came in 1888 with the introduction of the Wild Woodbine. Frederick Wills claimed the credit for both the name and the decision to go for the mass market to make the most of the company's huge new production capacity. Why Wild Woodbines? No particular reason, except that it suggested English country hedgerows – in reality, a far cry from both the American state of Virginia where the tobacco came from and industrial

Packing cigarettes at Wills No. 1 Factory in East Street, Bedminster, 1919

Bedminster where the cigarettes were made. But what's in a name?

The secret of Woodbines' success was overwhelmingly their price. When first introduced they cost five for an old penny and came in a paper sleeve rather than a cardboard packet. Frederick Wills used to say 'There's magic in a penny', and as a marketing ploy it certainly worked. For the next 60 years Woodbines, or Woodies or Bines as they were popularly known, were Wills' best-selling brand by far. Very little was spent on advertising – they sold in huge numbers simply because they were so cheap – and in the First World War almost every Tommy in the trenches had a packet of them in his pocket.

Factories in Redcliff Street were followed by newly-built factories in Bedminster and Ashton Gate. By this time Wills employed more than 2,000 people, although not just anyone could get a job there. The family had always been strongly religious and insisted that all female job applicants should provide suitable Sunday school references, pass a sewing test to prove their dexterity and sign a contract promising they would not 'contract matrimony within the said term, or play at cards or dice'. In return the company paid them well by the standards of the times and working hours were 'only' from 8 a.m. till 6 p.m. with the unheard-of perk of a week's paid holiday a year and an annual works outing. They also had a brass band, a savings bank, a theatre, a gym and a convalescent home by the sea in Clevedon. What more could they ask for?

1901 brought the outbreak of tobacco wars in Britain. A ruthless tobacco baron by the name of James B Duke came over from the USA bent on world domination of the trade. He walked into Players' boardroom in Nottingham and announced: 'Hello boys. I'm Dook from New York, come to buy your business.' Rather than roll over, the 12 biggest British cigarette manufacturers, led by W D & H O Wills, met on September 19, 1901 and formed the Imperial Tobacco group to do battle with Duke. But that's another story.

At one time or another, more than 30 members of the Wills family worked for the firm, but in 1963, with the retirement of Christopher Wills as sales research manager, the connection with the family was finally lost. Fast-forward to 1974, when Wills opened its giant new £15 million factory in Hartcliffe. It was built on a 57-acre site and was the largest tobacco factory in Europe, with its own supermarket, dentist, post office, bus station and six restaurants. At its peak in the late 1970s it

WILLS's *Wild Woodbine* cigarettes

W. D. & H. O. WILLS.

employed 4,500 people and produced 350 million cigarettes a week. It was a changing world, however, and after health scares and rationalisation, the Hartcliffe factory was closed in 1990. The offices became a rusting steel skeleton until in 2008 developers Urban Splash transformed it into 300 apartments and offices imaginatively named Lake Shore; the site of the factory proper became the Imperial Retail Park. Meanwhile, back in Bedminster, part of the main factory in East Street survives, and a smaller block in North Street has been turned into a restaurant and a bar, plus the popular Tobacco Factory theatre and arts complex.

The manufacture of tobacco products continued in a small way in a modern factory on Winterstoke Road, near Bristol City football ground, where Classic, Panama and Castella cigars were made until late in 2009. It was when this was closed and 75 jobs were exported to Spain that Bristol finally stopped making the product upon which

The factory in East Street, Bedminster, some of which has survived next to what is now a supermarket

The vast modern factory in Hartcliffe: opened in 1974, closed in 1991

so much of its wealth was based. Only the corporate headquarters remains, in one of the old red-brick tobacco factories in Upton Road, Ashton Gate where, of course, every member of staff has to obey the 'no smoking in public buildings' law. Times really have changed.

CIGARETTE CARDS

17

Made by Mardon, Son and Hall

THE FIRM OF MARDON'S really began in 1823 when John Price started a small printing and engraving business which was taken over by James Mardon in 1846. The company was still small and specialised in headed notepaper and address cards, but in 1860 it changed its name to Mardon, Son and Hall and opened a four-storey factory in Milk Street, making mostly cardboard boxes. It was in 1888 that it hit the jackpot when it signed a contract to make cigarette packets for W D & H O Wills, by then Britain's biggest producers of tobacco products. Not long after that, Mardon's added another product to its range – cigarette cards. The idea was to put a stiff piece of card inside every packet to ensure that the cigarettes were not bent or crushed. Then someone had the even better idea of printing thematically linked pictures on these cards, so that they became collectable and built brand loyalty. It was a marketing man's dream come true. W D & H O Wills were the first British cigarette manufacturer to cotton on. In 1895 they brought out a set of 25 cards with full-colour pictures of ships; after all, Bristol was a port, and sailors were enthusiastic buyers of cigarettes. The attraction of colour was powerful, since at the time newspapers had very few illustrations in black and white, let alone anything in colour.

There was one further refinement: why not write about the picture on the reverse side of the card? That way each set, usually of between 25 and 50, could become a miniature reference work, 'a poor man's encyclopaedia'. At a time when many people were barely literate and very few could afford to buy books, there was an argument for saying cigarette cards made smoking positively educational. They also successfully tapped into the British passion for collecting, and cigarette cards became almost as addictive as the cigarettes themselves for some. Children would wait around outside tobacconists asking customers 'Can I have your fag card, mister?'

Back in 1895 another set of cards featured Kings and Queens of England. They were an immediate hit and a set printed by Mardon's on silk was presented to Queen Victoria. After this, the company had to think long and hard to keep coming up with new subjects. Wills alone used more than 175 different sets, some with titles as obscure as Animals and Birds in Fancy Dress, Curiosities from Savage Lands, Instruments of Torture, Animals that Jump, Schoolboy Howlers, Queer Inventions and perhaps most obscure of all, Objects made from Captured Cannon. The choice of subject came to reflect the times. In peace time, cars, locomotives, wild flowers, dogs, insects, race-horses, cricketers, football players and actresses all featured prominently at various times. When the First World War started popular subjects switched to military cap badges, weapons, VC heroes, Bravest Deeds on Record, army regiments and warships.

This Factory at Warmley houses modern, high-speed Letterpress and Gravure printing machines

Mardons
OF BRISTOL
for Print and Packaging

Mardon's of Bristol offer a comprehensive printing and packaging service, including research, original design, high quality reproduction, printing by Litho, Gravure or Letterpress and an unlimited capacity for bulk manufacture.

MARDON, SON & HALL, LIMITED   TEMPLE GATE, BRISTOL. TEL. 24131

Similarly in the 1930s, when the Second World War was looming, a set of cards entitled Air Raid Precautions was very popular and the Home Secretary, Samuel Hoare, gave them his seal of approval with the words:

> I am responsible for a Home Defence scheme which might affect the life of any person in the country, and I therefore welcome these cigarette cards. I commend a study of these cards to your attention.

Cigarette cards had indeed become respectable. On the other hand, a set that featured British military aircraft, and on the reverse side their technical specifications including top speed, maximum operating height and so on was hastily pulped on government orders for fear that they might be useful to the enemy.

The choice of subject was not always straightforward. In 1914, Wills decided to produce a second series of cards entitled Musical Celebrities. Unfortunately then the First World War broke out and eight celebrities with German-sounding names were suddenly *persona non grata*. The offending cards had to be pulped, although some survived and are now worth thousands of pounds. Even the British royal family had to be wary of this strong anti-German sentiment and in 1917 changed its name from Saxe-Coburg-Gotha to the much more user-friendly Windsor. Similarly, in 1915, Wills brought out a set of cards to celebrate the centenary of the victory over the French at the Battle of Waterloo. The British government deemed this a tad undiplomatic at a time when the French were our firm allies in the trenches, and again the whole set was ordered to be pulped. One

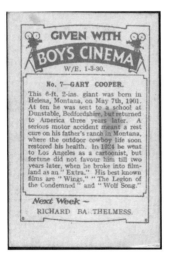

other set suffered the same fate – The Life of Edward VIII. This set had a very short life indeed when the king decided to give up his throne and marry an American divorcee, Mrs Simpson.

To illustrate these very diverse subjects Mardons employed up to 15 full-time artists and a number of freelancers. Often, two or three of them would work on a set of cards at the same time, each producing about ten illustrations a month. Very few were allowed to sign their work, although there were exceptions such as Arthur Wardle, who specialised in illustrations of animals, particularly dogs, and Peter Scott, painter of wildfowl and founder of the Wildfowl Trust at Slimbridge. Sample illustrations were sent to Wills and when these were approved the real work started. As for the text, Mardon's did all their research and copywriting in-house with the help of a reference library of more than 80,000 books. These were not much use when it came to contemporary sportsmen or film stars, however, and then researchers were dependent on press cuttings and popular magazines, which meant that errors occasionally crept in. Whatever the subject, the information had to be meticulously précised until the text totalled exactly 120 words for packets of ten cigarettes and 140 for packets of 20.

Mardon's prospered mightily and in 1902 became part of the Imperial Tobacco Company. In 1908 they built two huge new factories to cope with the demand for cigarette packets and cards. By 1922 they had 11 factories and by the 1930s they employed more than 5,000 people. During the Second World War, however, ten of their 13 factories were more or less destroyed by German bombs, the largest loss suffered by any company in Bristol. Besides, the production of cigarette cards was banned in 1940 as 'a waste of vital raw materials', and emphasis was switched to printing 13 million Ordnance Survey maps and packaging for troops' rations. After the war the company recovered to the extent that it had a total of 19 factories in Bristol by 1979 – but then a rival Canadian concern took it over, and the plants were gradually sold off or run down. Today all that remains is a factory in Tower Road, Warmley, currently owned by a company called Amcor, which continues to make millions of cigarette packets a year. The name of Mardon, Son and Hall, however, is long gone. Mardon's last set of cards for Wills, produced on November 22, 1955, was Life in the Hedgerows. When it was finished it marked the end of an important local industry – although for collectors at least, cigarette cards are not just a thing of the past.

COAL

18

Mined by the Bedminster Coal Company

IN THE MID-EIGHTEENTH CENTURY Bristol almost had it all when it came to the basic requirements for an industrial revolution, including two rivers, the Frome and the Avon, flowing through a major port enabling raw materials to be brought in and finished products exported. Above all, however, it was a major coal mining area, and it was coal that powered the industrial revolution. No wonder Bristol became a major producer of brass, glass, sugar, soap, pottery and lead. All of these industries consumed vast quantities of coal, and Bristol was sitting right on top of a huge coalfield.

The Bristol and Somerset coalfield runs from Wickwar in the north to the Mendips in the south. By 1750 the city had dozens of small collieries and by the end of the eighteenth century annual production reached somewhere between 400,000 and 500,000 tons. The coal seams around Kingswood, Hanham, Mangotsfield and Stapleton were the first to be mined, but during the 1740s a mining surveyor, Henry Bennett, concluded that the geological structures around Bedminster were very similar to those in north east Bristol and probably part of the same seam. Jarrit Smyth was the lord of the manor living in Ashton Court, and the Smyth family had owned most of the land around Bedminster, Southville and Ashton for generations. When Henry Bennett told Smyth about the fortune he could make by becoming a coal owner he jumped at the chance. In 1744 the Bedminster Coal Company was formed and the Smyth family received a handsome free-share or royalty on every ton mined beneath their land, while clearly never having to get their hands dirty.

In the following century there was a huge increase in demand for coal because of the many new industries in Bristol that had adopted steam power. By 1830, eighteen pits were in operation, the biggest being in Dean Lane, Southville, which employed more than 400 miners. Its coal was used for, amongst other things, the first steam ships to cross the Atlantic. Bedminster at that time was on the very edge of Bristol, and according to one account the coalfield was:

> situated in the midst of the most beautiful and rural scenery; verdure extends
> to the very pit mouths, and the tireless arm of the mighty steam engine, lifting
> like a plaything enormous loads out of the bowels of the earth, continually meets
> the eye as we clear a clump of trees or the brow of some flowery hillside.

A bit fanciful, perhaps, but Ashton Court is still only a 20-minute walk from Bedminster.

The shafts from the Bedminster coal mines were deepened and their underground workings extended until they eventually reached as far as Dundry, Temple Meads and

The pithead buildings in Ashton Vale with Clifton in the distance

Barton Hill and came within a few hundred yards of joining those of the Easton Colliery. Between 1850 and 1880 almost half the male population of the Bedminster and Ashton area worked down the mines, excavating the Bedminster Great Vein. One of them was a rough, tough character named Joe Wring who was so strong he had to have a special shovel made for him so he could shovel a hundredweight (112lb or 50 kilos) of coal at a time.

Conditions for miners like Joe were horrendous by modern standards. After being lowered in a cage from the pithead, often to a depth of 300 feet, they had to walk in a crouched position for up to two miles before they reached the coal face. There they worked for eight or even ten hours by the light of a flickering candle, using only a pick and shovel. In fact the coal seam was so thin and the roof of the tunnel so low, they were often forced to work lying on their backs, digging with just a short shovel. Temperatures underground were so hot that most miners chose to work in only a pair of old shorts. The coal they excavated was loaded onto wooden sleds, each weighing approximately a hundredweight, and hauled along the tunnel. The work was also highly dangerous, partly because most miners preferred to use candles rather than safety lamps. Candles, they said, gave a better light and the safety lamp, which was worn on a strap around their necks, often burned their chests. The danger came from gas such as 'firedamp' (methane) which could build up at any time and cause an explosion. In 1886 there was a massive one which killed ten men in the Dean Pit Lane mine. Eight others were badly burned or blinded. Compensation for widows, orphans or men disabled in such accidents was unheard of. Instead, as a mark of respect for the dead, the mine owners ordered the pit to be closed for a day. Very laudable – except that every surviving miner was docked a day's pay.

Bristol's coal miners were almost a race apart. In 1797 a report by Sir Frederick Eden mentioned that 'the colliers speak a jargon that is peculiar to them and perfectly unintelligible to a stranger.' Another report published in 1842 by Dr Leonard Stewart concluded that 'the colliers were generally uneducated and could not read or write and they commonly drink a good deal, particularly on Saturdays and Sundays. They generally keep a good deal together and marry among their own people, having usually large families.' It was not just men who worked in conditions like

The South Liberty Colliery

these. Dr Stewart interviewed an 11-year-old boy named George Raikes who had started work at the age of nine. 'He stated that there were boys of seven and eight working in the pit. He himself began work at 6 a.m. and finished at 4 or 5 p.m. He found it rather hard work and gets tired sometimes.' George Raikes clearly had a talent for understatement. The report went on to say:

> Boys were used in opening and shutting doors to regulate the current of air. They worked 12 hours a day and received 4d a day. Slightly older boys were employed on piece work to drag the coal along the cramped tunnels using a belt and harness attached by a chain to a cart or sled.

The Children's Employment Commissioners were clearly concerned. One, Elijah Waring, commented:

> I was induced to examine closely into its effects on the frame, conceiving it to be a barbarous way of applying muscular power. But when I consulted with the underground manager of Sir J Smyth and Co, he aptly compared the boys to young horses whose shoulders were first broken to the collar.

Another commissioner wrote:

> One boy says he is 13 but only looks nine or ten years of age. With another boy he draws two hundredweight of coals at a time. Says he eats 'whatever he can catch'; does not go to the Sunday School because he has no clothes other than those he works in. Earns 6d a day; his brother earns 2s 6d a week in the same

pit. He sometimes works the night shift for an extra 6d. Cannot read. Never had a pair of shoes or stockings in his life. Had once worked in the pit three days without food.

There were, and still are, huge reserves of coal beneath Bristol. A royal commission report published in 1864 calculated that there were 6,104,310,982 tons (just over 6 billion) still waiting to be mined, although how they could make such an exact calculation is anyone's guess. This, they said, was enough, at the present rate of production, to keep the Bristol coalfield busy for the next 6,000 years. By 1905 this figure had been reduced to estimated reserves of 6,083,600,000 tons, and the expected lifespan of the pit had plummeted to a mere 2,858 years. These, of course, were wildly optimistic miscalculations – and over and above that, there was a problem. Bristol coal was found only in very thin seams, two or three feet thick, trapped between layers of hard rock, and these seams often disappeared completely or continued but not horizontally. This meant that the coal was difficult and expensive to mine and unsuitable for the new cutting machines being introduced in northern mines. In the face of this competition local coal owners were slow to modernise, so much so that a Newcomen pump engine installed in the South Liberty pit in 1750 was still in use in 1895 and possibly the 1920s.

As a result, the Bristol coal industry declined rapidly at the beginning of the twentieth century. In the 1870s the average annual output was 524,156 tons, enough to supply almost all of the city's needs. By 1900 this had slumped to 43,697 tons. The first mine to close was Ashton Vale Colliery, in 1906 when 186 men were thrown out of work. The closure of the Dean Lane Colliery followed soon after, in 1910. Partly out of pity for the miners, Dame Emily Smyth paid for them to clear the site and turn five acres of it into a park, which was subsequently named after her. Nowadays there is nothing left of the Dean Lane pit except for a set of railings, formerly a bandstand, which marks the top of the area's biggest pit. It is strange to think that beneath modern central Bristol there is still a maze of dank, disused tunnels, most of them full of filthy black water.

Today, coal is imported on a vast scale from all over the world into Royal Portbury Dock. Ironically, it is then carried on a specially reopened branch line up the Avon Gorge and through Bedminster, passing over the defunct mines that used to supply all of Bristol's needs; but who knows what will happen when the world's oil reserves are exhausted? There might come a time when Bristol's coal mines are re-opened.

CONCORDE

19

Made by British Aircraft Corporation

CONCORDE 002, THE FIRST CONCORDE built in Bristol, made its memorable maiden flight on April 9, 1969. Thousands of people converged on Filton to watch it take off and millions watched it live on television. Many Bristolians took time off work. As well as the general public, workers from the British Aircraft Corporation lined one side of the runway and those from Rolls Royce, who made the immensely powerful Bristol Olympus 593 engines, lined the other. According to that day's *Evening Post*, 'they witnessed one of the technological triumphs of the 20th century'. Shortly after 2 p.m. the chief test pilot Brian Trubshaw started the aircraft's four engines. There was a touch of drama as a glitch arose with engine number four. A senior design engineer wrote later: 'I noticed, as did Brian Trubshaw, that one engine did not fully light. But there was no turning back. He just kept on going.' The aircraft slowly taxied to the Gloucester Road end of the runway with its distinctive droop-snoot nose angled down. There it paused for final checks and then the moment had come to take to the air for the first time. Throttles were fully opened and reheat ignited. The noise was ear-splitting and the ground shook. At 2.48 p.m. precisely it lifted off, and the great white bird was in the air. It flew only 22 miles to Fairford in Gloucestershire, where it made a perfect landing in front of 10,000 people. Trubshaw told the waiting press: 'It was wizard – a cool, calm and collected operation. It was a very precise aircraft to fly.'

What he did not mention was that the plane's altimeter had failed, but he had managed to make a perfect landing despite the fact that he was sitting at the controls 35 feet above the runway when he touched down, relying on his skill and pure guesswork rather than his instruments. The *Evening Post* continued to rise to the historic occasion:

> Concorde may have given us the runaround over the years, smitten us with fits of panic, temperament, wrath and fear, but 002's first take-off into the blue today makes all men love her.

Michael Heseltine, Minister for Aerospace at the time, described it as 'The biggest single leap forward in flying since the first flight of any aircraft'. In a way he was right.

Concorde ▼ *Leadership*

**With the Concorde supersonic airliner,
Britain and France lead the world.**

Leading the British programme on Concorde—designed,
developed and manufactured in collaboration with Sud-Aviation—
is the Filton Division of

BRITISH AIRCRAFT CORPORATION

BAC 94   ONE HUNDRED PALL MALL LONDON SW1

The world is about to be halved in size

Concorde
AEROSPATIALE (SNIAS) FRANCE & BRITISH AIRCRAFT CORPORATION

Concorde was the world's first supersonic airliner. It could cruise at 1,350 mph or 25 miles a minute, which is more than twice the speed of sound and faster than a bullet from a rifle; and all this at a height of 60,000 feet, or 11 miles. At this enormous speed it 'expanded' by six to 12 inches because of the heat generated, which reached 127ºC. The speed enabled Concorde to fly from London to New York in only 3 hours 20 minutes, compared with the Boeing 747's seven hours. Flying west, it arrived comfortably before it left, according to the clock, at least.

The design and building of Concorde was an enormously complicated and problematical business. The cost of developing the aircraft was at first estimated to be £150 million. As usual this proved a woeful underestimate; in fact the figure was a billion, maybe even £1.5 billion. Altogether, more than 50,000 people worked on the project at one time or other. The English and the French co-operated up to a point, but the language barrier was a formidable obstacle. (The writer of this book had the unenviable job of trying to teach French aeronautical engineers working at Filton some basic English. Most of them either could not or would not learn. To be fair, the British were probably at least as inept at learning French. As one British engineer put it: 'If we couldn't find a way round the language barrier, we just barged through it.')

There were other formidable problems. The British design drawings always used Imperial measurements (feet and inches), the French, needless to say, used metric. In addition, the project threw up some interesting cultural differences. At meetings the French favoured long, abstract discussions. The British were more to the point and down-to-earth, and the French thought they were not 'serieux' enough. Another interesting difference: one meeting ended with agreement between the British and French executives and the leader of the British group said 'Jean, just so that both sides are clear on what has been agreed, why not get Honorine in and dictate a note on the subject?' Jean replied 'D'accord, mais qui est Honorine?' (All right, but who is Honorine?) Honorine was the secretary who had worked for Jean for three years, but he knew her only as Mademoiselle Dupont.

Until very late on, the two sides could not agree on a name for their revolutionary aircraft. The British wanted to call it the 223 (the Bristol type number), arguing that numbers are the same in any language (which of course, they are not when spoken). The French disagreed. The British then came up with SST, short for Supersonic Transport. The French again disagreed, because the order of the letters was not the same in French. They suggested TSS instead, short for Transport Supersonique, but of course that was unacceptable to the Brits. The French then came up with the Super Caravelle, because the Caravelle at the time was one of their modest successes, albeit one based largely on the design of the British Comet. This was another non-starter, and there was deadlock until one fateful Sunday in January 1963 when a British executive involved in the project had a family discussion about it over lunch. His son looked through a

battered copy of *Roget's Thesaurus* looking for synonyms for 'agreement', to emphasise the fact that it had been a joint project, and came up with 'concord'. The French warmed to the idea, but only if it could be spelled their way, with an 'e' at the end. 'Mais non,' said the British, until a few years later, in December 1967, the then Minister of Technology Anthony Wedgwood Benn, finally let them have their way.

An interesting subplot to the Concorde story was Russia's clone version, the TU 144, which the British press dubbed Concordski. It bore an uncanny resemblance to Concorde, which was not perhaps surprising when it was discovered that an electrical engineer at Filton, James Doyle, had secretly sold copies of Concorde blueprints to the Russians for the relatively meagre sum of £5,000. Doyle, code-named Ace by his Russian handlers, changed his name to Jimmy Cameron when he was unmasked in 1999 but was never convicted of industrial espionage. The Concordski project effectively ended in disaster when the first production aircraft crashed in front of 200,000 onlookers at the Paris Air Show in June 1973, killing all six people on board and eight on the ground. Brian Trubshaw had been invited to fly in it that day, but had thankfully declined.

BOAC ordered seven Concordes, doubtless after a lot of behind-the-scenes pressure from the British government, and Air France ordered four. Unfortunately, by this time the world aviation market had changed. What airlines wanted was a slower transport for the masses, in other words hefty, wide-bodied Leviathans like the Boeing 747, which could fly at only a third of the speed of Concorde but carried four times as many passengers. Despite the sales team's best efforts, the 74 options to which 16 different airlines had signed up were dropped. The last Concorde to be made in Bristol left Filton in June 1980.

Concorde's viability for BOAC and Air France was delayed until it finally came into service on the key trans-Atlantic route. This was largely because the Americans

A French Concorde on fire as it takes off from Charles de Gaulle Airport, Paris on 25 July 2000. It crashed moments later

were not keen on the idea of a European aircraft putting one over their own aircraft industry. Endless legal objections were raised to the plane landing in Washington and New York, and high-level political pressure had to be used before the go-ahead was given. Even then, the aircraft's profitability was always a vexed question, although many wealthy people on both sides of the Atlantic became regular passengers. Joan Collins often used to fly on Concorde between London and New York, and to ensure that she did not have to talk to a stranger she would book two seats, at a cost of £8,500 each for a one-way flight. But she did not fly as often as an American, Fred Finn. He was on the first and last Concorde flights and holds the Guinness World Record for the most journeys as a passenger. Between May 26, 1976 and October 24, 2003 he flew a total of 718 times. At one time he would make at least two return trips a week between Heathrow and New York – and all of them in the same seat, 9A, at an estimated cost to his company of more than £2 million. In 2008, when he visited Concorde 216 at Filton and sat in his favourite seat, he commented: 'It's a great shame that she's not still in the air. What they've got at Filton is something very special; it brings back a lot of memories for me.'

The beginning of the end for Concorde came on July 25, 2000 when an Air France Concorde crashed into a hotel soon after take-off from Charles de Gaulle airport. The 109 people on board were killed, and four on the ground. All Concordes were grounded on August 16 while the cause of the crash was investigated. Investigations eventually concluded that a sharp piece of titanium debris left on the runway by an American DC10 that had just taken off burst one of the Concorde's tyres and then fractured a fuel tank, causing a massive fire in one of its engines. After extensive modifications costing £280 million, service was resumed on November 7, 2001. But the great white bird's race was run. On April 10, 2003, British Airways and Air France jointly announced that they were going to retire Concorde for good. The aircraft had

The final flight of Concorde 216 over the Clifton Suspension Bridge on November 26, 2003

been in service for nearly 30 years, but the airlines said the cost of keeping it airworthy was just too great. Cheekily, Richard Branson, boss of Virgin Atlantic, made BA an offer of £1 per aircraft, but they said no.

The last big occasion for Concorde was its leading role in the flypast over central London on June 4, 2002 to celebrate the Queen's golden jubilee. Its last commercial flight from New York to London was in October 2003 and the Bristol-built Concorde 216 made its last emotional return to Filton on November 26. It was the final flight of any Concorde in the world and after 5,639 supersonic flights, the final landing. Thousands of Bristolians packed the area of the Clifton Suspension Bridge, the Downs and Filton as it flew in low from the south west before finally touching down at 1 p.m. Many had tears in their eyes.

Concorde might have been one of the noisiest and most uneconomic aircraft ever to fly, but it was also arguably the most beautiful machine ever made. In March 2006 it was voted the greatest British style icon of the twentieth century, ahead of the London underground map and the Spitfire. Now Concorde Alpha Foxtrot is still in a hangar at Filton. But her fate is uncertain and largely in the hands of Airbus UK. In the words of retired Senior Design Engineer on the Concorde project, Doug Douglas,

It can't be right. Bristol's greatest technological achievement and her brightest star deserves better.

CORRUGATED IRON

20

Made by John Lysaght Ltd

JOHN LYSAGHT WAS BORN IN COUNTY CORK in 1832 but was sent to Bristol to be educated. At school he became best friends with a boy whose father, John Clark, owned a small business on Temple Back making galvanised buckets. In 1857 Clark died and left the business to his son, but for some unaccountable reason he was not particularly interested in buckets and very generously gave the business to John Lysaght. So at the age of 24, the young Irishman was in business, employing six men and a boy whose total wages were £7 a week. Soon after that he expanded his product range to include portable galvanised bath tubs, which were very popular with Victorian manual workers whose houses definitely did not include an inside bathroom.

A few years later John Lysaght hit the jackpot when he started making galvanised corrugated sheeting in a new works, which he called St Vincents, by the side of the Feeder Canal. This four-acre site had originally been used by a company that had built most of the machinery used in Brunel's ss *Great Western* but had since gone bankrupt. Corrugated iron was originally invented by the London architect and engineer John Palmer in 1828, but Lysaght developed and sold it so successfully that by 1864 his workforce had increased to 29, and by 1878 to 400. Two years previously he had bought another 13-acre site just down the road, which he called his constructional engineering department. Here he made farm buildings, exhibition halls, cricket pavilions, railway stations and churches, all using galvanised corrugated iron.

In 1878 he bought the Swan Garden Iron Works in Wolverhampton. This guaranteed him a steady supply of iron sheets which came to Bristol via the Gloucester and Sharpness Canal and the river Avon to be finally unloaded from the Feeder Canal. Lysaght's then galvanised and corrugated the sheet metal and sent it on barges the short distance back to the city docks. From here, 90 per cent of it was exported all over the world, as far away as China and Peru.

Lysaght's business really took off when he started shipping his corrugated iron sheeting to Australia on a massive scale. The huge demand resulted from a gold rush which led to thousands of migrants leaving Britain in a hurry, hoping to get rich quick. When they arrived in Australia, many were so intent on panning for gold that they had no time to build a conventional house, preferring to erect a more or less prefabricated one made of corrugated iron. It meant thousands of people sailed to Australia with their houses stowed away in the hold. Each component was numbered for easy and quick assembly, rather like a Victorian version of IKEA flatpack furniture. Lysaght's also exported shops, hotels and churches, or as one Australian historian noted: 'Anything from a pigsty to a cathedral.' At the height of the gold rush, more

JOHN LYSAGHT, Ltd.,
ST. VINCENT'S WORKS, BRISTOL,
MAKERS OF
Galvanized, Corrugated, and Flat Sheet Iron,
NETTING, BUCKETS, ROOFING, GIRDERS,
And General Constructional Work.

JOHN LYSAGHT. Limited.
NETHAM IRONWORKS.
BRISTOL.

than 30,000 corrugated iron building kits were exported in a single year. These original houses are now worth a fortune, and great care is taken to preserve them. Locals think they are as Australian as kangaroos, but they were in fact made in Bristol.

John Lysaght, like many others, made his fortune not from gold but from supplying the needs of those searching for gold. A testament to the fortune he made was the 'castle' he built in 1891 in Silverthorne Lane, St Philips, which is still there today. It was originally designed by his brother Thomas with the help of a local architect, Milverton Drake, and was clearly intended to impress. The style, in the words of the architectural historian Tim Mowl, is 'Ruritanian Romanesque', characterised by 'self-inflated grandiosity'. The offices and meeting rooms used by Lysaght's are palatial, with Doulton tiles, mosaics and the extensive use of mahogany. Since 2000 the building has been used by a firm of engineering consultants, Garrad Hassan, undeterred by the fact that the landing is apparently haunted by 'half a dog'(which half is unclear). The workshops, just across the courtyard, were by contrast hot, dirty and noisy. They were partly burned down in October 2006, when many of the props used by Aardman Animations were destroyed, and the building is still a charred shell.

In addition to corrugated iron, Lysaght's had a 'country department' which produced sheep feeders, pig troughs and the like and exported vast quantities of wire netting and linked fencing to Australia, where it was famously used to keep rabbits, kangaroos and wallabies away from land grazed by cattle and sheep. In 1879 John Lysaght visited Australia, by far his biggest market, and quickly decided that his three

A Second World War Anderson shelter made from Lysaght's corrugated iron

selling agents were not up to the job. He started his own manufacturing company there, the Victoria Galvanized Iron and Wire Company, and left two of his sons in charge. They originally used the brand name Orb but in 1897, perhaps for sentimental reasons, they changed the name to Redcliffe. Their father had died two years earlier, at the relatively young age of 63.

At the beginning of the First World War, the German army occupied Liege, the third largest river port in Europe. It was the European destination for most of Lysaght's products and on August 7, 1914 the company called a meeting of its 1,000 workers at the Netham works and broke the news that they would all be on short time. According to company history at least, there were no protests but only cheers and hurrahs for King and country. Within weeks many of those men had signed up for the Somerset Light Infantry and were fighting in the trenches.

In 1920 John Lysaght's Bristol business was bought by the giant steel company GKN and the company weathered the Depression – just. The good times returned in February 1939, eight months before the start of the Second World War, when the government foresightedly ordered 250,000 Anderson air raid shelters, each made of 14 panels of galvanized iron easily bolted together. They were distributed free to families earning less than £250 a year, and cost all others £7. During the Second World War many Bristol women working for Lysaght's built, among other things, Bailey bridges and Crusader tanks, as well as anti-aircraft guns and shells. Later on, the company was heavily involved in the construction of the Mulberry Harbours and

Corrugated iron was used for many different types of building. This tin tabernacle was one of the more unusual

the Pluto (Pipe Line Under The Ocean) project that made the D-Day landings possible. In 1951 the company came to specialise in oil drums, after it merged with the American company Robert Rheem. The name Lysaght's lingered on in Bristol until the early 1970s when it finally disappeared. A sad end but at the height of its fame legend has it that:

> there was scarcely a building in the Empire which was not in some part constructed from Lysaght's corrugated iron.

Made by Unity Corsets and Fantasie Foundations

THE CORSET INDUSTRY REALLY STARTED early in the nineteenth century, when fashion demanded that women should have an hour-glass figure – whether they had the body for it or not. The ideal was to have a waist that could be spanned by two (men's) hands. According to a contemporary commentator:

> Ladies must know how to hide all the defects in the proportions of the body and must be able to mould the shape by the stays so as to preserve the intestines, that while she corrects the body she may not interfere with the pleasures of the palate.

You could choose from a variety of styles. Some corsets were designed for wearing during the day, others during the evening. Later in the nineteenth century some were even especially designed for cycling or playing tennis. But it was not just women who had to be shoe-horned into these whalebone creations. Even girls were put into corsets, or 'improvers', designed to enhance their posture as well as their shape. 'Let the corset do all the work,' was the guiding principle – so much so that it was allegedly a pleasure to wear, because 'its sensations were so agreeable that those once addicted to it would rarely abandon it'.

One of the most successful Bristol manufacturers, Langridges Corsets, was started in 1830 by George Langridge in a small workshop in Totterdown. He went for the top end of the market, specialising in very expensive corsets with hand-embroidered designs in silk. The business rapidly expanded and soon moved to a new factory in Temple Street, and it was at this time that he invented the trademark Unity and soon after that started making crinolines. In fact he claimed he invented the crinoline, but that was doubtless just sales talk. Besides, as an invention, the crinoline had its drawbacks. Its rigid skirt-shaped structure with a semi-rigid whalebone hem meant that sitting down could be a real problem. If the wearer failed to spread her skirts out properly, the entire contraption would fly up in her face.

Early Unity corsets were very rigid and consisted of as many as 60 pieces of material reinforced by lengths of whalebone. The most popular colours by far were dove grey and black. As whales became hunted almost to extinction the price of whalebone became prohibitive and steel stays were used instead. The company was eventually taken over by two partners Messrs Ryall and Sherrif and the factory was moved to St George and then, in 1920, to Two Mile Hill in Kingswood. Mr Ryall was convinced that 'there must always be a corset industry to give control to female figures' and embarked on a programme of expansion to prove it. He exhibited his company's

products at the Trade and Industries Fair in London in 1923 and allegedly caused a great stir in the corsetry trade with their use of Celanese satin and a choice of five colours.

At the Kingswood factory there was a strange division of labour. The cutting was done almost exclusively by men, while the women did the sewing. Conditions for both sexes at the factory in Two Mile Hill were said to be primitive, with one central stove on the ground floor supposed to heat both floors of the large building. Business boomed, however, and within ten years of its opening four extensions were built. In 1930 a new, larger factory was built in Waters Road and ten years later, when Mr Ryall died, his son Charles took over the business.By this time the company had changed its name to Fantasie Foundations and Charles Ryall shocked the traditionalists in the company when he made the decision to 'throw the last rigid corset out of the window'.

During the war corsets were considered far too frivolous and inessential, and the factory was turned over to the mass production of uniforms and parachutes. One worker, Kathleen Burnham, later described what it was like:

> I started work when I was 14, in 1939. After six months we had to change from corsets to making parachutes, gas mask cases and gun turret covers. Queen Mary came to visit us in the factory. She spoke to me, she said: 'I expect you say Oh bother it! when things go wrong' because we had the parachutes all laid out around us. That was nice of her. We worked from eight in the morning to six o' clock at night. If we had to get up in the night to go down into the air raid shelter, which most nights we did, we were still expected to be on time next day. If we were three minutes late, a quarter of an hour was stopped from our pay.

In the early 1950s the company was still going strong and proudly proclaimed, 'Today Fantasie Foundations hold a pre-eminent position in the field of all-elastic light-weight corsetry while by no means neglecting the requirements of the figure requiring firm control. Nowadays there is still the same optimism, the same faith in the future'.

To prove how far into the future they were prepared to move Charles Ryall applied, in 1956, for a patent for a new type of multi-functional panti-girdle which amazingly was designed to flatten the stomach, lift the bottom and act as a suspender belt, all at the same time. In those days such a garment was worn by perfectly slim teenage girls as well as their less slim mothers and was sold with the irresistible slogan, 'Happiness is a flat tummy'. Moving very rapidly with the times they even produced a new girdle designed to be worn with hot pants.

In those days many workers at the factory virtually had a job for life or, as the company publicity department put it, 'many workers are now employed in the Fantasie Foundations factories whose families have identified themselves with the fortunes of the company over the past fifty years and there are others whose working life has

covered almost the entire existence of the company and who are now on the list of pensioners.'

But innovations such as the panti-girdle didn't stop the decline of the company. Fantasie Foundations became Bentwood Lingerie which specialised in underwear for Marks and Spencer. But the running down of the corset industry was inexorable and when the factory finally closed down in 2001 the last vestige of a once thriving Bristol industry died with it. But for a few years at least some grandmothers with fuller figures all over the country will probably go on wearing them.

22 FAGGOTS

Made by Brains

NOBODY IS QUITE SURE WHERE the word faggot comes from. Some say it derives from the Welsh 'ffagodau', which roughly translated means a mixture. It is also a word for a bundle of dried sticks used to start a fire. Crucially, it also came to mean the meat balls sold by butchers up and down the country. These were traditionally made from anything they had left over at the end of the day, in particular pigs' offal – liver, kidneys and heart plus a bit of stomach lining, all mixed with breadcrumbs and seasoning and wrapped in caul fat, again from pigs' innards. Despite what some people seem to think, there were never any brains in Brain's faggots.

The name came from Herbert Hill Brain, born in Bristol in 1864, the son of a grocer on the Gloucester Road. He started his own grocery wholesale business in 1890 in Temple Street. It thrived and in 1927 he bought new, bigger premises in Upper York Street, where he specialised in curing and smoking bacon and cooking hams. In 1925

one of the company's employees suggested that instead of just selling pork products he should make something from the leftovers, more specifically faggots. Brain agreed, and gave his perhaps unfortunate name to the new product. He reputedly never tired of telling people that while no, there were no brains in his faggots, many other parts of the pig found their way there, in particular liver and rind. To these ingredients are added onions, cornflour, tomato purée and seasoning; in other words, they are a kind of cross between mince, meatballs and haggis. The packet also contains what is described as 'a rich West Country sauce', or gravy to you and me. They are an acquired taste, though not for vegetarians. Neither are they really suitable for people on a diet. They are very high in fat – 12.5 grams in just two faggots – and also in carbohydrates. Served with mashed potatoes and peas, they are certainly filling. They come in packets of four, but it is a very hungry person who can eat more than two at a sitting. One commentator on a website admitted:

If I'm honest, half of the pack usually ends up in the dog.

Herbert's two sons, Arthur and Leslie, followed their father into the business, but though the family link has now been lost, the name lives on. Nowadays they're called Mr Brain's faggots, the 'Mr' presumably giving the product a more traditional feel, in the style of Mr Kipling and his exceedingly good cakes. The company says 100 million

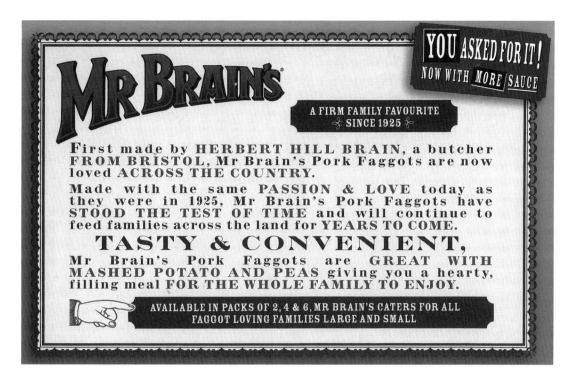

faggots are made, and presumably eaten, every year. Eventually the firm was bought by the Irish conglomerate Kerry Foods which makes, among many other products, Homepride flour, Wall's sausages and Matteson cooked meats. Kerry claim that with the Mr Brain brand they now have a 99 per cent share of a £10.7 million market. On April Fool's Day in 2003 the factory in Bridge Road, Kingswood closed with the loss of 250 jobs, and Mr Brain's faggots are now made far away in County Durham, though allegedly still with that West Country sauce.

An interesting postscript: a 2004 radio commercial featuring Mr Brain's faggots had a story line with a husband challenging his wife's repetitive routine of a set meal for each day of the week. He wanted lasagne, but was told that as it was Friday, he was to have faggots as usual.

> I've nothing against faggots, I just don't fancy them

he wailed, and as a result the advertisement was banned for breaching the rules of good taste and decency. As noted earlier, faggot is a word with many different meanings.

23 FLOUR

Made by Henry Jones

HENRY JONES CAME TO BRISTOL from Monmouth in 1803 determined to make his fortune. Success did not come overnight, but within a couple of years he had opened a bakery at 37 and 39 Broadmead, in premises previously owned by the Western Biscuit Bakery. There he experimented with a new and very different way of baking, without yeast. Eventually, on March 11, 1845, Jones was granted a patent for what he described as 'self-raising flour', and with uncharacteristic modesty he averred: 'My flour will not excite criticism of the most gastronomic individual.' He then set about selling his new product, and to do that he indulged in energetic and shameless social climbing. In 1846 he joined the most fashionable hunt in the area, the Duke of Beaufort's, and made a point of mentioning his patented flour to the Duke himself while waiting for a fox to break cover. Next day he followed this up by sending a case of his flour by special delivery to the Duke. His hard sell worked, and soon after that he received this letter from the Duke's chief cook:

> Dear Sir,
> You will please to send on receipt of this two cases of your excellent flour; one is for His Grace (the Duke of Beaufort), the other is for Lord Adolphus Fitzclarence. His Grace has spoken to him and he wishes me to show his man how to work it when on board the Victoria and Albert yacht with her Majesty. Lord Adolphus Fitzclarence is the Commander, (so) by that means her Majesty is sure to eat bread made from your flour. Send both cases to me at Beaufort House. I hope you are quite well.
> Remaining yours truly, William H Turnham.

With contacts like that, Henry Jones and his self-raising flour were well on their way, and less than six months later he was granted a Royal Warrant as a purveyor of patent flour and biscuits to Her Majesty. Jones continued to push his product with energy and flair. An advertisement soon after asked the question:

> Why is Jones' patent flour like the sun? Because they are both original and self-raising and their beneficial effects are alike appreciated in the Palace and the cottage.

In 1846 an article in the medical journal *The Lancet* referred to 'the contribution to public health and to the daily comfort of the masses made by self-raising flour'. It was not long before Jones received an American patent, and the first gold medal for the new

Henry Jones's shop and bakery in Broadmead

flour was issued in 1852 to an American firm in Chicago using Jones's self-raising flour.

The next step was to persuade the Admiralty that fresh bread baked with self-raising flour could make all the difference to the diet of sailors who up until then had to be content with stale, weevil-infested bread. Jones claimed his concern for the health of British service-men prompted his energetic promotion of his product as much as profit. Fortunately for him, the two just happened to coincide and some influential people were easily persuaded. James Hosken, captain of the ss *Great Britain*, told Henry Jones:

> Having tried the flour you sent me during her last voyage, I have a great pleasure
> in stating that it made the best bread I have ever seen at the table of the Great
> Western or the Great Britain and I shall be glad to hear you succeed in bringing
> it into general use at sea, particularly for long voyages.

Their lordships in the Admiralty took their time, but years later, and with the help of a recommendation from Florence Nightingale, Henry Jones finally persuaded the Royal Navy to use his self-raising flour on board its ships. By the time his patent ran out after 15 years, he had made a fortune. He then went on to make a second one from another of his inventions – arrowroot biscuits. Henry Jones had indeed come a long way from his roots in Monmouth, but in his old age he returned home to the other side of the Severn and lived in Court House, Caldicot, until he died in 1891 at the age of 78.

GLASSES

Made by MW Dunscombe

Dunscombe's on the corner of St Augustine's Parade and Denmark Street

SPECTACLES WERE FIRST MADE IN BRISTOL in 1797 by a Mr Jackson at a shop on St Augustine's Parade, which in those days was a bustling quayside. This was not such a strange place to make spectacles since they are of course lenses and lenses are used in ships' telescopes. Mr Jackson prospered in a small way and was eventually joined in business by his son-in-law John Braham, who took over the firm in due course. In 1855 he took on a 14-year-old apprentice, Matthew Dunscombe, from East Street in Bedminster. The boy had no great education but made up for it by his ambition and willingness to learn. While working at the firm's wholesale business in London, for example, he studied French in his spare time at King's College and was awarded a certificate for his endeavours. In 1863 John Braham died and his sons and nephews took over the business, but they did not have the drive or acumen of the former apprentice. In 1874, at the relatively young age of 34, he bought the firm and changed its name to M W Dunscombe and Company.

In the early Victorian period, when windows were small and candles and later oil lamps were the only form of lighting, it is easy to imagine how difficult it was for many people to read, let alone sew. It meant Matthew Dunscombe was on to a winner when he started manufacturing spectacles on a relatively large scale. Other firms were selling them, of course, but most were of inferior quality since anyone could set themselves up as an optician. Dunscombe's spectacles were different. His advertisements boasted: 'The lenses used by M W Dunscombe are of the finest quality optical glass and Brazilian pebble (a colourless quartz). The spectacles are unsurpassed for utility and moderate price. Dunscombes – the only spectacle manufactory in the West of England.' Later on he produced some of the first bifocals made in this country, with 17 steps in the manufacturing process.

Matthew Dunscombe was not just interested in making money out of people's defective eyesight. He also researched into the workings of the eye and published a book titled *Vision and Spectacles*. In addition he became a founder member of the British Optical Association and an avid collector of antique specs, so much so that his collection is now in the safe-keeping of the Science Museum in London. He was also a member of the Royal Meteorological Society, which might partly explain his firm's becoming a manufacturer of barometers and nautical instruments. In his old age he became a leading member of Bristol's Freemasons – not bad for a boy from Bedminster who left school at 14.

Matthew Dunscombe was a man of considerable energy. Three of his seven children, including his improbably named eldest daughter Adeliza Amelia Clara Mary

Elizabeth Emma Frances, joined the family firm. (According to his great-grandson Peter Dunscombe, all the names were suggested to Matthew by his wife for him to choose from. To save argument, he opted for them all, but it must have cut down on the couple's choices when other daughters came along.) His son Ernest was responsible for extending the company's product line to cameras and all things photographic, and this led to the firm making magic lanterns, in effect Victorian slide projectors. Before electricity, these were lit by limelight or heated quicklime. Sadly Dunscombe's lantern shows, drawing on a library of more than 20,000 slides, were forced to close after two village halls in the Bristol area were razed to the ground as a

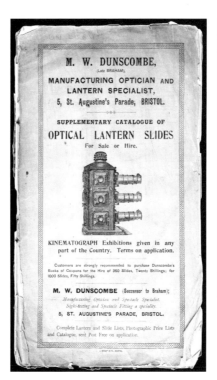

Matthew Dunscombe

result of accidents involving extremely hot limelight. At around the same time the firm started a monthly journal for amateur photographers, *Photographic Chat*.

In the early 1930s two of Matthew's grandsons, Kenneth and Max, joined the business. Kenneth showed considerable initiative when he went off to Jena in north Germany, the centre of the European lens industry, and wrote a thesis on contact lenses (in German); this led to Dunscombe's becoming a pioneering prescriber of contact lenses in this country. The photographic business also grew, and a small 'cinematograph theatre' was opened for home movie makers. It is now a kebab shop on the Centre.

In 1938 an American descendant of the Dunscombe family, Ernest Fear, having made his fortune in Kansas City, visited his home city of Bristol. While here he fortunately commissioned Dunscombe's to make a colour film of Bristol, and this eventually became the only film record in colour of the Bristol Blitz. Fear showed it to any Americans willing to watch in his effort to persuade the USA to join the war, and it is now the property of the BBC in Bristol.

The Dunscombe family connection with the firm was finally lost when it was taken over by the opticians Batemans; but they are still trading today, although a few doors away from their original premises, and as as a link with the old days, the word 'OPTICIANS' is still written on the shop on the corner of Denmark Street where it all first started.

25　HATS

Made by Christy

John Wayne

A BIT OF LICENCE IS NEEDED to include Frampton Cotterell, just north of the M4, in a book about Bristol, but hat making, or more specifically felt hat making, was for a long time a cottage industry in the north Bristol area. The Cotwolds from the Middle Ages had produced wool on a huge scale, and since Flemish émigrés had introduced the art in the sixteenth century, many villages in South Gloucestershire had made felt hats using rabbit fur, chopped wool, mercury and size. In 1773 Miller Christy began making felt hats in Bermondsey, east London, but in 1812 the firm he founded opened a factory in Park Lane, Frampton Cotterell, where the skill of felt hat making was still very much alive – and wage rates were far below those in London. The factory was big by the standards of Frampton Cotterell, with two long three-storey buildings sited in such a way that the windows on both sides gave plenty of light. Individual workers were responsible for cutting and shaping the hats, and in 1834 more than 120 people were working in the factory, making some 1,300 hats a week. Over the years, tens of thousands of their wide-brimmed felt hats were exported from Bristol docks to the sugar cane plantations of the West Indies, where protection from the sun and tropical rain storms was needed by the workers.

An interesting footnote to this piece of local history was recently unearthed, involving an American by the name of John B Stetson (1830-1906). He saw and liked the wide-brimmed and high-crowned hats made by Christy so much that he decided to make his own version in St Joseph, Missouri, but with beaver rather than rabbit fur. He named it the Stetson or ten-gallon hat, and in 1865 he started selling it with the slogan: Boss of the plains. Christy's were furious and sued Stetson for infringement of their patent. Research by a Bristol University lecturer, John Moore, has discovered that J B Stetson fought a long patent case with them – and lost. The result was that he had to pay a licence fee to market the famous Stetson hat. The Stetson company could certainly afford it, especially after their hats were worn by every cowboy in every Western film ever made, usually white ones for the goodies, black ones for the baddies. If you go to the website of the modern Stetson Hat Company, though, you will find no mention of Miller Christy or Frampton Cotterell.

Christy's came up with two more variations on the theme of the wide-brimmed hat – the one that Boy Scouts traditionally wore until quite recently, and the one still worn by the Canadian Mounties. In addition, plantation owners and their wives also became customers when 'beaver' hats became fashionable. These were made from lambswool, with trimmings made from beaver fur, but they went rapidly out of fashion when silk hats or toppers replaced them in the middle of the nineteenth century.

The original factory in Frampton Cotterell

Conditions for the workers in Frampton Cotterell were hard and dangerous. A highly toxic mercury compound was used in the felt making process, and the windows were kept closed at all times to prevent the rabbit fur from blowing about. As a result of breathing in the poisonous mercury fumes over a long period, workers were prone to loss of memory and violent mood swings, and ultimately became 'mad as hatters'.

The factory was finally closed by Christy's in 1864 and their manufacturing base moved to Stockport in Cheshire, though the up-market title Christys' of London was retained, the eccentric punctuation being theirs, not ours. The company is still going strong in Witney, Oxfordshire where it makes fur felt hats as well as top hats, panamas and even felt baseball caps. The family connection with the original family ended in 2007 when the former chairman John Christie-Miller died, aged 96.

The factory buildings in Frampton Cotterell were turned into a Roman Catholic convent, and eventually private houses. The one nearest the road is called The Old Hat Factory, but that is all that is left of an important but unhealthy local industry.

26 HOT AIR BALLOONS

Made by Cameron Balloons

Don Cameron

opposite:
the busy interior of the Cameron Balloons factory in Bedminster

DON CAMERON, A GLASWEGIAN, studied aeronautical engineering at Glasgow University and then at Cornell University in the USA before coming to Bristol primarily because it was, and still is, the centre of the British aircraft industry. For a time he worked on fixed-wing aircraft but in 1966 he and a few friends founded the Hot Air Group. Together they made the first modern hot air balloon in the basement of Don's house in Cotham, and named it the Bristol Belle. To demonstrate how serious they were about flying balloons, they insisted that they should be given a special licence, and the first ever pilot's licence rated for hot air balloons only was issued to D Cameron of Bristol soon after that. The Bristol Belle still exists, and although somewhat moth-eaten by now, it is occasionally inflated for old time's sake.

Don started making balloons seriously when he moved his business into an old church hall in Cotham in the early 1970s. He had noticed that crowds immediately gathered whenever he started to inflate his balloons, and when they were airborne he was convinced that they had huge commercial potential as mobile overhead advertising hoardings. To attract publicity, and because he loved flying balloons anyway, he went in for a number of stunts or world firsts. He flew over the Sahara and the next year crossed the Alps, despite being warned that it was impossible. After that, his balloons kept getting bigger and the flights more and more ambitious. His most famous and most serious to date was the Breitling Orbiter 3, the first balloon to travel round the world non-stop using a combination of helium gas and hot air. It was as high as the Tower of Pisa, its envelope had the volume of seven Olympic swimming pools and it weighed as much as a modern fighter plane. Taking off on March 1, 1999, it landed 19 days and 22 hours later in Egypt after travelling 28,431 miles. The pilots were Bertrand Piccard (Switzerland) and Brian Jones (UK).

The company moved in 1983 to a much bigger building in Bedminster, an old Robinson's print works. Today it employs about 70 people in Bristol and another 28 at an American sister company. It is an informal place to work, with many employees multi-tasking. Don's daughter Hannah, for example, is a director of the company who trains pilots as well as doing the public relations. Cameron Balloons have become by far the largest manufacturer of hot air balloons in the world, making on average one every two days.

For many Bristolians, Cameron Balloons are closely linked with the annual Balloon Fiesta at Ashton Court, and the sight of the most outlandish shapes floating silently over their heads, interrupted only by the occasional blast from the propane burners. To say Cameron balloons come in various shapes and sizes is a considerable under-

statement; they are often positively weird, from a Disney fantasy castle to Bertie Bassett made up of various liquorice allsorts, a Tesco shopping trolley, Donald Duck, a Burger King hamburger, a pair of Levi jeans, Action Man, a Harley-Davidson motorcycle, a Chubb fire extinguisher, Rupert Bear, Thomas the Tank Engine and the head of Darth Vader. The shapes are so extraordinary that it is easy to forget that they are made only of fabric, with no hidden metal structure. For advertising purposes, balloons must be very hard to beat. The flying saucer made to launch the DVD of the sci-fi movie *Independence Day* made the front page of practically every national newspaper.

To date, Cameron Balloons have built more than 600 of these fantastic creations, and all have been certified as airworthy aircraft. The largest number of passengers that have flown in a balloon

is 50. That was achieved in Holland in a balloon built by Cameron Balloons in 1988. At the opposite extreme, a one-man balloon has the pilot suspended in a harnessed seat instead of a basket. A conventional balloon costs about £17,000, and the fuel for one flight is about £25 – a small price to pay for a ride in one of the most impractical but fun forms of transport ever invented.

In December 2007 Don was awarded Freedom of the City of Bristol. At the time, the Lord Mayor said:

> Bristol is now recognised as the ballooning capital of the world due to Don's vision, ability, enthusiasm, commitment and hard work.

His company now exports 85 per cent of its products, and thanks to Don Cameron, Bristol to many people is synonymous with hot air balloons and ballooning.

ICE CREAM

Made by Verrecchia's

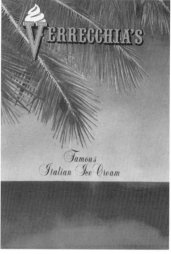

ITALIANS PRONOUNCED IT 'VERRECKIA', Bristolians preferred 'Verreesha', but however mangled the pronunciation, the Verrecchia family was famous in Bristol for more than 70 years for making and selling its own very special ice cream. Eugenio Verrecchia was born in 1880 in the small mountain village of Valvori, between Rome and Naples. At that time southern Italy was desperately poor, and expatriate Italians living in Scotland sent word back that money and jobs were relatively plentiful there. Eugenio decided to join them, but there was one big problem: he had no money for his fare. With only a limited knowledge of geography, he decided the only thing to do was to walk. He set off, taking any job he could get to pay his way. It cannot have been easy; he was illiterate and did not speak a word of any language other than the Italian dialect of Valvori, which was almost unintelligible outside the village.

On landing in Britain, Eugenio made his way to Glasgow, mainly because of its thriving Italian community; many of his countrymen had got as far as Greenock on their way to America, but decided to stay put in Scotland instead. He stayed in Glasgow for some time, returned to Italy in 1910 to marry a local girl, Domenica Stefano, and in 1911 went back to Scotland with his new wife. He applied for British naturalisation, describing himself as a musician, which stretched the truth a little; his only musical ability involved turning the handle of a barrel organ.

Eugenio and Domenica then had seven children in quick succession, and in 1925 they moved south to Bristol, probably because a number of other immigrants from Valvori had settled here. The Verrecchias moved into a small house on Coronation Road, Bedminster and it was soon after that that Eugenio turned his hand to ice cream making, planning to sell it in a small shop on Peter Street, near Bristol Bridge. (Sadly that old area was flattened in the Blitz and is now buried under Castle Park.) He might still have spoken very little English, but he knew how to publicise the opening of his new business – by offering everyone a free ice cream. Crowds gathered and mounted police had to be called in to control them. Verrecchia's ice cream was on its way.

Soon after that the family opened a factory in Brislington, followed by an ice cream parlour in East Street, Bedminster. The design of this was a straight copy of a parlour recently opened in Sunderland, and Eugenio even persuaded the carpenter who had made the cubicles up there to do the same for him in Bristol. The formula worked; before long, on sunny days at least, people were queuing round the block to buy Verrecchia's ice cream.

By this time the family was almost totally anglicised; but on June 10, 1940, the day Mussolini declared war on Britain, Churchill issued the order 'Collar the lot', and

The shop on St Augustine's Parade with 'an ice-cream machine on wheels'

thousands of Italians, including complete innocents such as Venezio, Eugenio's second-youngest son, were interned on the Isle of Man for the duration of the war. For some reason the rest of the family were left in peace, apart from a few stones being thrown through the windows of one of their parlours. Despite this, Eugenio always remained intensely grateful to his adopted country. As for Venezio, he returned to Bristol and opened a very successful café on St Augustine's Parade.

After the war the Verrecchias hit on a radically new idea. For most Bristolians, East Street, Bedminster was too far away if they simply wanted an ice cream – so why not take the ice creams to them? To make this possible, the family designed what they called 'an ice-cream machine on wheels', or an ice-cream van, as we now call them. It had a more or less hand-built body attached. The advantages were obvious: 'It means that ice cream is made only minutes before it is served. Each morning the vans will leave with a complete load of ready-mixed ice cream and will not have to return to the depot for refills.' The idea caught on rapidly, and decades later, by 1993, Verrecchia's had 36 vans appearing in parks and on street corners all over Bristol.

Almost the whole family worked in the business. Eugenio's son Roberto, for example, started and ran the factory in Stockwood Road, Brislington. His brother Romeo and his wife Maria built up the fleet of vans, which toured the city seven days a week. (Romeo married Maria – known as Mrs V to thousands of customers – in 1946.) The vans thankfully carried the Verrecchia name, rather than a silly newly-coined moniker

Verrecchia ice cream makers at work at the Stockwood Road, Brislington factory, 1960s

like Mr Whippy. In the long, hot summer of 1976 they sold on average 7,200 cornets and 18,000 lollies a day. To their great credit, the Verrecchia family also took on and beat the big national companies Wall's and Lyons Maid, who wanted a monopoly of ice cream sales in small local shops.

Asked at the time why Verrecchia's ice cream was so special, Betty Verrecchia, who was company secretary, said simply: 'Because it's traditional, home-made stuff'. Incidentally, Betty and her sister Gloria found time to play the accordion and piano respectively, and they can be seen playing a duet in the Oscar-winning film *The English Patient*. They did not have a difficult audition; the director of the film, Anthony Minghella, was Betty Verrecchia's nephew and Gloria's son.

Domenica died in 1971, and Eugenio in 1973. Eventually, for reasons still not entirely clear, the family decided to close the factory in the 1990s. Betty said at the time:

> None of us could bear to see the factory merged or taken over. It's been in the family so long. I suppose it's a bit of excessive pride.

Whatever the reason, Verrecchia's melted away like ice cream in the sun.

28 JUKE BOXES

Made by Chantal Ltd

ACCORDING TO ONE EXPERT, the Chantal Meteor in the 1960s was 'the most stylish juke box ever made in England – a radical changer mechanism allied to a cabinet straight from The Jetsons makes this the most desirable of all juke boxes.' (The Jetsons were a space-age cartoon family on American TV, the flip-side of The Flintstones.) The Chantal Meteor was made, believe it or not, in Bristol, or to be more precise, Kingswood. The original Meteor was designed and made in Lausanne by a Swiss engineer called Jean Foufounais and named after his wife Chantal. The British version was redesigned in Kingswood by another engineer, David Fry of the chocolate family, and made to look far more stylish; the Swiss, after all, might be good at cuckoo clocks and army knives, but when it came to juke boxes they were not exactly world leaders.

But why not import direct from the real home of the juke box, the USA? The answer is that in the 1950s there were strict import restrictions which made this difficult and very expensive, so it was much better to make our own. For a time Chantal Ltd did very well and the Meteor sold in large numbers – perhaps as many as 500, maybe more. Each one cost the same as a semi-detached house, but it offered a choice of 100 seven-inch 45s, or 200 sides altogether. It was the first juke box in the world to have such a big selection, and for the pubs and clubs that bought them they were real money-spinners. If each record cost 6d (2.5p) to play, they could theoretically pay for themselves in a couple of years.

The problem was that the redesigned Chantal Meteor was a triumph of form over function. They looked wonderfully futuristic with various weird protuberances, a Perspex bubble cover and loads of fluted chrome – but they were not really suitable for heavy everyday use and were always breaking down. One large operator can remember setting fire to as many as 50 of them at the same time because he was so fed up with them not working.

In 1960, to make matters worse, a fire broke out in the factory in Small Street, St Philip's where they were being assembled, and many finished juke boxes as well as most of the components were destroyed. It was the beginning of the end, and the company folded two years later. Nevertheless, nowadays Chantal Meteors sell for up to £7,000 to nostalgic sixty-somethings desperate to recreate their lost youth. It's just a shame that very few of them remember that Kingswood, of all places, was an international style capital of contemporary youth culture.

29   LEAD SHOT

Made by William Watts

IT MAY OR MAY NOT BE TRUE, but the story goes that in 1780 a Bristol plumber by the name of William Watts was wending his way back from a pub near his home, sat down to rest in the churchyard of St Mary Redcliffe and promptly fell asleep. Perhaps as a result of divine inspiration he had a vivid dream in which his irate wife was pouring molten lead down on him from the church spire, through one of her kitchen sieves. Because it fell vertically from a great height and landed in puddles, it emerged in the form of perfectly spherical balls of lead. He woke the next morning, more sober and determined to find out whether his dream could be made into money-making reality. In 1782, after some experimentation, he came to the conclusion that it was the height from which the liquid lead fell that was crucial. Too short a fall meant that it ended up tear-drop shaped. He therefore took out a patent for 'making small shot solid throughout perfectly globular in form, without dimples, scratches and imperfections'.

Watts' house on Redcliffe Hill, demolished 1968, with its specially-constructed shot tower

Now all he had to do was put his invention into production. To this end he took out a lease on a house on Redcliffe Hill, opposite the churchyard. Then, in 1786, he added a three-storey Gothic-style crenellated tower at one end 'to remind citizens of the prospect of Westminster Abbey' according to Watts, but also to give him the height to work with. Internally, he cut a hole through all the floors and dug down into the sandstone below ground level until he broke through into the Redcliffe Caves; now, finally, he had a vertical drop of 90 feet.

Using lead from the old Roman mines on the Mendip Hills, heating it to 400°C and pouring it in molten form through a perforated zinc tray, the globules then fell, cooling and hardening all the time until they were collected in a tank of cold water at the bottom, perfectly spherical. The only problem was that at high tide the tank in the basement was flooded with sewage-laden water from the docks, and his neighbours complained about the stench. He retaliated by saying their pigs smelled much worse. Watts's fortune was now assured, and a local poet even celebrated his success in very bad verse:

Mr Watts very soon a patent got
So that very soon only himself could make Patent Shot
And King George and his son declared that they'd not
Shoot with anything else and they ordered a lot.

With that kind of fame and adulation he was able a few years later to sell up to a local firm for £10,000, which in those days made him the equivalent of a multi-millionaire. Unhappily, he invested the money in a number of failed business ventures, including the building of Windsor Terrace in Clifton in 1792, and ended up bankrupt.

Lead shot continued to be made in the factory on Redcliffe Hill, and in 1883 a visitor described the process, which had not essentially changed since Watts's time:

Windsor Terrace, Clifton

> On reaching the summit of the tower we entered a moderately sized square apartment, the walls of which are crusted over with a foul greenish deposit, a mixture of sulphur and arsenic. In the centre of the room is a large melting pan full of boiling metal, around being pigs of lead and a variety of tools required in the work. Beside the boiler is a pen trap door, over which one of the workmen presently places an iron stand. On top of this is securely fixed what is aptly termed a colander, some 20 inches in length and about a foot wide, perforated at the bottom with innumerable small holes, according to the size of the shot to be manufactured. On the surface of the molten lead and arsenic arises a thick scum which acts as a kind of filter, allowing the fluid metal to pass slowly through the small holes at the bottom in drops.

A modern health and safety officer would clearly have closed the works immediately, but another Victorian observer merely noted:

> The molten lead is falling like a magnificent cataract of sparkling silver, while the sound from beneath, as the myriad of drops fall into the well, somewhat resembles that of a distant fusillade.

Watts's historic house and factory were demolished in December 1968 to make way for the dual carriageway that links Bedminster with the St Mary Redcliffe roundabout. The strangely shaped shot tower near St Philips Bridge that replaced it was made redundant in 1994, so Bristol's links with the plumber's alcohol-fuelled invention are now conclusively severed.

30 LEATHER

Made by Thomas Ware and Sons

Thomas Ware's tannery on Clift House Road, Southville

THE ORIGINAL THOMAS WARE was a miller, farmer and tanner who was born in 1790 in Devon and died in 1873. Many of his descendants still live in the Bristol area, among them Edward Ware, the property developer, but none is involved in tanning. In 1840 Thomas's son Wallace built a tannery on a five-acre site in Clift House Road by the side of the Avon in Southville, and the business became a limited company in 1890. Clift House was originally the dower house of Ashton Court, standing on the site now occupied by the Riverside Garden Centre.

Douglas Brearley, the father of the present managing director, Marcus Brearley, came originally from Halifax and was taken on as an apprentice at Thomas Ware's in 1930. He never retired but continued to work there until his death in 2003, aged 92, by which time he was managing director, a Merchant Venturer and a highly respected member of Bristol's business community. There must be something compelling about tanning, because Marcus has himself worked for 47 years for the firm and remembers wandering about the tannery when he was as young as eight. His son Alistair now also works for the company, making it three generations.

After the last war there were seven tanneries in Bristol, mainly supplying local boot and shoe factories. Thomas Ware and Sons is the only one left, specialising in leather for the soles of high-quality shoes. They have recently started marketing Dri-Wear – 'a sole leather which wears superbly and withstands the vagaries of the British weather' – while one of their biggest customers is Church's Shoes of Northampton, now owned by Prada. Church's charge high prices (between £250 and £410) for their 'very, very well-made shoes' for gentlemen: 'Look after a pair well and they will last you a lifetime.' Thomas Ware's leather is also used in brief cases, handbags, saddles, stirrups and bridles, policemen's gun belts, cricket ball covers, billiard cue tips and most recently leather floor tiles selling at £600 per square metre! Until recently they also supplied a manufacturer of paraphernalia used for various kinds of bondage.

The tanning process is long, complicated and occasionally smelly. It starts with the purchase of ox hides, the skins of dead beef animals, usually about a hundred at a time. The hides, still clearly straight off a dead bull or cow and in various permutations of black, white and brown, are piled up in the first shed. They have already been weighed, trimmed and salted – the sprinkling of salt preserves the hide for up to six months. There was a time when the hair on the hide could be used for making carpet underlay, and the flesh for fertilizer and gelatine which in turn was used to produce cosmetics and even ice cream. Unfortunately, since BSE most of the hair and flesh have to be thrown away at the considerable cost of £67 a ton, although some is used

The first stage: hides just arrived from the slaughter house

The interior of the tannery, with its series of pits, which Marcus Brearley describes as 'antediluvian'

Marcus Brearley proudly displaying some of his finest quality leather

to make organic compost.

The next process, liming, consists of immersing 55 hides at a time in pits. They weigh approximately two tons altogether but this increases to five tons when they are fully soaked. These pits each contain 3,000 gallons of various liquids which are constantly kept moving by electric motors. For the first 24 hours the hides are immersed in three pits full of water to wash the salt out, and are then moved into pits of a lime solution which swells them and loosens the hair. The process then calls for suspension in more pits, each filled with different solutions of tanning liquor. It takes more than three months from the time the raw hides arrive to when they eventually emerge as fine leather. English oak bark was the original raw material used in the tanning process, but this is now practically unobtainable. Thomas Ware use an exotic mixture of mimosa from the acacia tree from South America or South Africa, chestnut from Italy or Slovenia and the myrabolan nut from India. This comes in sacks in dry powder form, and about 50 tons of it are used a month.

When you visit Thomas Ware's, the smell is probably what you remember most of all. At the start it is the rather putrid whiff of the raw hides, but at the end it is the wonderful, strong and unforgettable smell of pure, best quality leather. The tannery could be described as Victorian, but Marcus Brearley prefers antediluvian, which takes us back a few more millennia than the nineteenth century. Whatever, there was a time when tanning was one of Bristol's major industries. Now only Thomas Ware and Sons are still going, employing 50-plus people and carrying on a very traditional but thriving industry.

Made by Limbs & Things

PUT VERY SIMPLY, if you are training to be a doctor, nurse, midwife or paramedic, it's very difficult indeed to find a patient who is willing to let you practise on them. In particular, trainee doctors need to learn how to diagnose, dissect, inject and sew up using models of various body parts, so it does not matter too much if, inevitably, they get things wrong the first time. Enter a small but rapidly expanding Bristol company called Limbs & Things, which makes and supplies different body parts, or 'training models or simulators' as it calls them.

Margot Cooper started the company in 1990. She is an Australian who was brought up on a farm and so was used to seeing the occasional dead animal. From an early age she was fascinated by how their bodies worked, and at school she actually enjoyed dissecting dogfish, frogs and sheeps' eyes. This eventually led to her becoming a medical illustrator, drawing graphic illustrations of every part of the human anatomy for use in text books. In 1990 she put this knowledge to good use when she started Limbs & Things in Bristol. She had come to the conclusion that medical training using patients or animals was often not possible or suitable. In particular, human patients were becoming much more aware of their rights, and resistant to the idea of being used as guinea pigs. Her answer was to start making highly realistic models of body parts with extremely accurate anatomical details. The advantage of using them was that teaching and learning could be done away from patients, hospitals or operating theatres. In fact the company supplies training kits complete with CDs, so that students can teach themselves techniques and skills in their own time, practising over and over again until they get it right. 'The useful thing about our products is that it enables students to get over the embarrassment, and practise in private before having to handle a real patient,' says the sales director.

Products made by Limbs & Things range from a toe with a very nasty looking in-growing nail, strap-on breasts complete with various lumps and bumps that can be easily inserted or removed so that male doctors can practise breast examination on each other, a translucent uterus, a prostate gland, limbs with cuts and gashes that need to be stitched and whole torsos which can have tubes inserted into various orifices. The research and development department at Limbs & Things is particularly proud of the touchy-feely material it created, which looks and feels exactly like human skin and soft tissue. One student doctor is even said to have fainted when an incision was made in the 'skin'. Previously, trainees were forced to use pigs' trotters because they were cheap, and pig skin was similar to human's. The problem was that after a few

Margot Cooper with some of her
Limbs & Things products

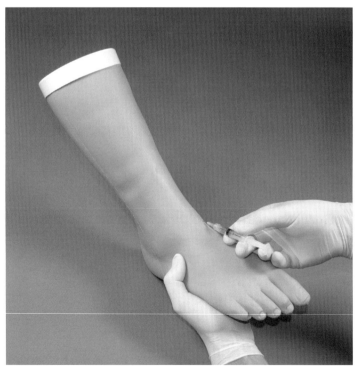

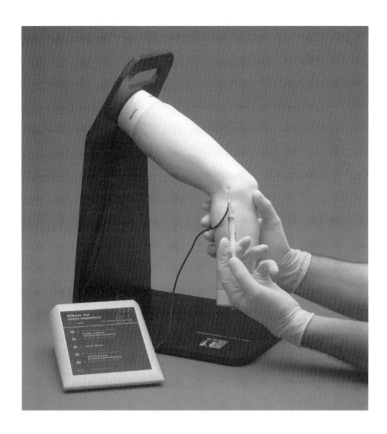

hours, the trotters started to stink.

Limbs & Things are constantly developing new products, including various add-ons or additional features to the innumerable parts of the body they make. These can be inserted so that advanced medical students, including trainee keyhole surgeons, can be faced with unexpected surprises and complications. The products are exported all over the world, although this sometimes causes problems. The strap-on breasts, for example, were deemed unrealistically large for oriental markets, while the size of the penis, used for practice in inserting a catheter, gave some male students a complex and had to be reduced.

From its nondescript-looking headquarters on an industrial estate near the council's waste recycling centre in St Philips, Limbs & Things now employs more than 80 people. It has won international prizes, including two awards for 'special contribution to medical education'. It has branches in the USA, Australia, Sweden and Germany, and over 50 per cent of its products are sold all over the world. Twenty years after she founded the company, Margot Cooper now takes more of a back seat and leaves the day-to-day running to the managing director, Nic Riley. She has though conclusively proved that thanks to Limbs & Things, 'the movement away from using patients is on a roll'.

32

MOTORCYCLES

Made by Douglas

Before they made motorcycles, Douglas made drain gratings

WILLIAM DOUGLAS CAME FROM GREENOCK in Scotland, where his family were members of the Douglas Hamilton clan – hence the tartan on the petrol tanks of some of their bikes. With high unemployment in Glasgow, William came south to Bristol in search of work and got a job in Kingswood, repairing boot-making machinery in a town that at the time had dozens of footwear factories. His brother Edward soon joined him and together they rented a house and small workshop for £16 a year. In 1882, with borrowed capital of £10, they started up in business as the Douglas Engineering Company. The £10 bought them a portable forge, a vice and a grindstone, and they started work as blacksmiths. They worked hard, and they were able to repay the £10 in full after only three months, which must have appealed to their Scottish frugality. Soon after that they opened a small foundry in Hanham Road and started to produce lasts for the boot and shoe industry; from these they diversified into manhole covers, drain gratings and lamp posts, but they were still ambitious and recognised that the internal combustion engine was the coming thing. In 1907 they collaborated with Joseph Barter, an engineer from Bedminster, and fitted one of his horizontal twin-cylinder engines on to a standard bicycle frame. The resulting contraption might have been a bit Heath Robinson, but it worked – and it was the start of something much, much bigger.

Their first serious motorcycle was a 200cc flat twin-cylinder copy of a French motorcycle called the Fee (French for 'fairy'). Between 1907 and 1910 they went on to produce a 350cc machine of their own design, which by the standards of the day was seriously fast. In 1910 they started racing their motorcycles and only two years later they won the Isle of Man Junior TT and the Grand Prix of France. For the next 20 years they more or less dominated motorcycle racing, and the publicity helped make Douglas a major name on two wheels. During the First World War the Douglas factory expanded rapidly after it received big government orders. It produced over the next four years more than 70,000 motorcycles at the rate of 300 a week, most of them the Douglas WD 2.75 hp 2-speed model, to be used by the army's despatch riders from the frozen tundra of northern Russia to the deserts of Persia.

After the war the Douglas factory had plenty of work re-conditioning thousands of ex-army motorcycles and repainting them shiny black in place of dull khaki. The company also produced the first 500cc motorcycle to exceed 100 mph. It has to be said though that Douglas motorcycles at this time were not

A Douglas motorcycle from the early 1920s with a 350cc, 2¾ hp engine

below: the factory at Douglas Road, Kingswood

particularly reliable, as quality and workmanship were never really their strong points. Despite this somewhat dubious reputation they won a great publicity coup when they were given a royal warrant by George V. The king was probably too overweight ever to hoist himself astride a motorcycle, but it is certain that his sons Henry, Duke of Gloucester and the Duke of York, later George VI, rode around on Douglases. It made the marque something of a two-wheeled status symbol, for a time at least.

Unhappily, the firm was never well managed, and in the 1920s unpaid tax bills of between £5 million and £10 million almost bankrupted the company, along with a disastrous fire in 1926. It managed to pull back from the brink and in 1928 started building a specialist machine for the new and very popular sport of speedway, called at that time dirt track racing. This brought a lot of favourable publicity as well as sales, and in the late 1920s the company was employing nearly 3,000 workers and even had its own sports ground, which was used years later by Bristol Rovers. More favourable publicity followed in 1933 when Robert Edison Fulton Jr wrote a book entitled *One Man-Caravan*, in which he described how in 18 months he rode 25,000 miles – or more or less around the world – on a Douglas fitted with car tyres.

At this time William Douglas was still in charge, together with his two sons. His daughter Rosie was also a motorcycle enthusiast and even as a young teenager was often seen riding far too fast down Kingswood High Street, sometimes standing up with her feet on the saddle. The Douglas family, it seems, could get away with more or less anything because, as one local historian remarked, 'As the Ewings were to Dallas, so the Douglases were to Kingswood'. In 1932, however, the Douglas family left the company and William Douglas died in 1937, aged 78. During the Depression the company diversified into trucks, cars and aircraft engines. The car looked promising

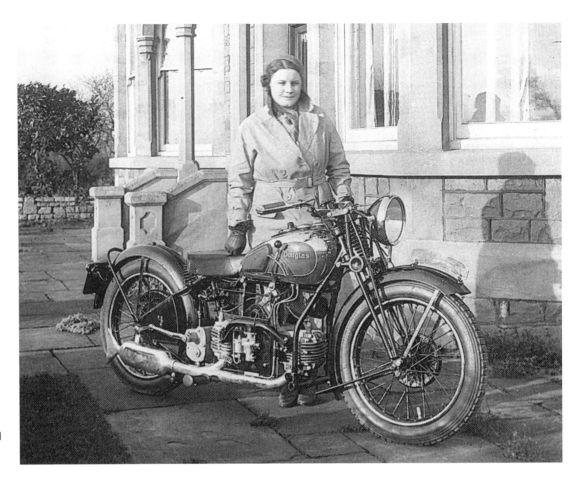

Rosie Douglas and motorcycle outside the Douglas family home in Kingswood

at first, but only six were ever built. Typically, the company overreached itself, and in 1935 it was in financial trouble again and was renamed Aero Engines Ltd after being bought by businessmen who wanted to build Hispano Suiza engines under licence. Instead of that, as so often happened, the Second World War brought a major reprieve, with the company again working flat-out to produce munitions, parts for fighter planes and mobile generators. After the war Douglas turned to making a range of electric delivery vans, but by 1948 they were in trouble yet again. The directors decided to go back to their core product and produced a series of motorcycles based on a 350cc flat-twin engine, but they sold only moderately well. In 1955 they announced with a great fanfare the 350cc Douglas Dragonfly – the bike that was going to turn Douglas round and return the company to full production and profitability. It was not to be. The Dragonfly certainly looked quite modern, even stylish, and it handled reasonably well, but road tests revealed that it was not as fast as it looked; at low revs it did not have enough power, and its top speed was an unimpressive 75 mph. Some 1,600 were built altogether, and although a 500cc prototype was shown in 1951, it never made it into production. In the post-war years, the Douglas family's direct links with the company

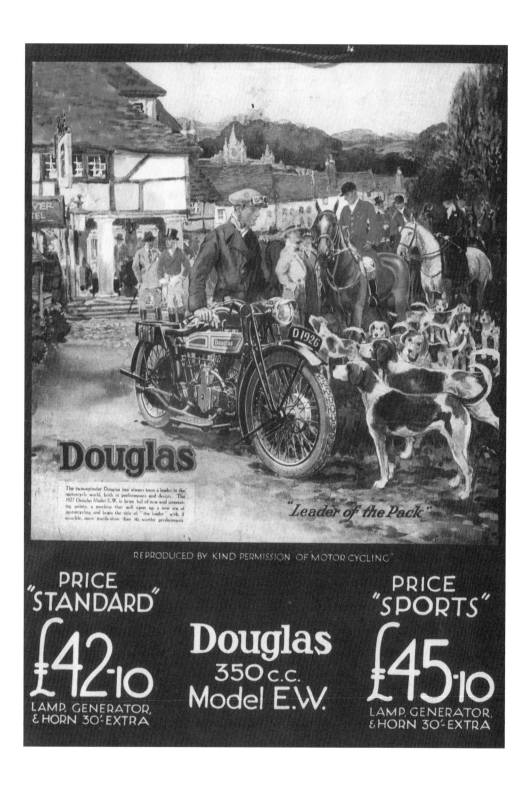

The twin-cylinder Douglas has always been a leader in the
motorcycle world, both in performance and design. The
1927 Douglas Model E.W. is brim full of new and interesting points, a machine that will open up a new era of
motorcycling and bears the title of "the leader" with, if
possible, more justification than its worthy predecessors

Douglas

"Leader of the Pack"

REPRODUCED BY KIND PERMISSION OF MOTOR CYCLING

PRICE
"STANDARD"
£42·10
LAMP, GENERATOR,
& HORN 30ʹ EXTRA

Douglas
350 C.C.
Model E.W.

PRICE
"SPORTS"
£45·10
LAMP, GENERATOR,
& HORN 30ʹ EXTRA

Two Douglas motorcycles, one an 0W1 from 1934, the other a 1919 frame with an experimental V4 engine

might have been lost, but in 2007 William's great-grandson Bill described how he had inherited his family's passion for motorcycles:

> There were second-hand Duggies all over Bristol in those days,   going for next to nothing, and in about 1948, when I was 13 or 14, a group of us clubbed together to buy an old pre-war thing to ride in Hanham Woods. We hid it in the bracken and rode it to destruction. We just kept riding it as long as the engine kept going. You could buy a two-gallon can of petrol for a shilling. We didn't worry if anything else went wrong – and that included the brakes.

In the early 1950s the writing was on the wall. The company was eventually purchased by Westinghouse Brake and Signal, and the new owners were more interested in making Vespa scooters under licence. Motorcycle production ceased in 1957 and the Duggie, as it was affectionately known, was finally laid to rest.

MUSTARD GAS

33

Made by National Filling Factory No. 23

ON THE EVENING OF JULY 12, 1917, German artillery fired shells into the British trenches at Ypres; but instead of being filled with high explosive, these shells contained a brown, oily fluid. It had a revolting smell, something like rancid garlic or mustard, but apart from that it did not seem particularly dangerous, causing only slight irritation to the eyes and throats of the British troops. During the night, however, they began to feel searing pain, and gradually suffered swelling and huge blisters up to a foot long wherever their skin had come into contact with the noxious fluid. By the next day, the results were horrendous. All the troops affected lost large patches of skin, and in some cases the fluid burned through the skin to the bone below. Many were also blinded, a lot died from the massive damage done to their throat and lungs, and most survivors never fully recovered their health and died young.

The British code-named this new chemical weapon HS, for 'Hun Stuff', but its rank smell inspired another name that stuck: 'mustard gas'. Its formal name was dichloroethyl sulphide, and although it was called a gas, it was in fact a potent, oily fluid that could penetrate thick clothing, boots and even masks. It persisted for a long time before vaporising, unlike other gases used in the war. It would freeze during the winter and still be just as toxic when it thawed in the spring. Its long-lasting properties are confirmed by French and Belgian farmers who are still occasionally suffering chemical burns after stumbling across rusty mustard gas shells ploughed up on old battlefields.

A German soldier, plus his dog, prepare for a British gas attack, First World War

British casualties of gas warfare

When this new German weapon was first used, the outcome of the First World War was very much in the balance. As a result, in October 1917, the government took the decision to fight like with like and start producing British mustard gas, and for better or worse, it chose Avonmouth to be the main centre for this new and extremely dangerous chemical warfare industry. The factory, on the western side of Chittening Road, was given the innocuous-sounding name of National Filling Factory No. 23. Progress on building it was slow, and finally ground to a halt in March 1918, when a strike stopped work. The government then decided to cut its losses and paid the Kings Weston Estate £20,000 for some land bordering Kings Weston Lane.

No planning permission or lengthy public enquiries were needed, so within a few months a massive new factory was built, using some of the equipment from Chittening Road. It spanned Kings Weston Lane, with offices and a hospital on the south side of the road, the former, for some strange reason, vaguely resembling a French chateau. Notices were put up all around Avonmouth, forbidding the picking of blackberries within a mile radius, and a sickly wild garlic smell hung permanently in the air. Production soared to the point where 20 tons were being produced a day, and eventually, just

German troops in 1918 ready for a British mustard gas attack. By then 25 per cent of all British shells contained mustard gas

before the armistice was signed, 125 tons a day. By this time 25 per cent of the shells fired by the British army were filled with mustard gas.

Because the gas was obviously designed to be as dangerous as possible, and health and safety were a relatively minor consideration, the plant's chief medical officer had his work cut out. Some 1,100 people worked there in conditions that were appalling by modern standards. Mustard gas inevitably spilled onto the wooden floors, where it soaked in, and levels of contamination rapidly built up. In addition, workers had to make do with non-flushing toilets, woefully inadequate washing facilities and poor lighting and ventilation. No wonder as many as a thousand workers were sometimes off sick at any one time, and on two occasions the whole factory had to be closed down because of 'operational difficulties'. In December 1918 the chief medical officer reported that in the six months that mustard gas had been produced in Avonmouth, 1,400 serious illnesses had been recorded, including three fatalities. Some workers had 'three or four attacks', and the sickness resulting included 'blisters on every part of the body, conjunctivitis, bronchitis etc and chronic effects of debility, cough, gastric pain and breathlessness'. All were directly related to the lethal substance the plant was manufacturing.

Meanwhile, the factory at Chittening, after many delays, was up and running. Workers, many of them local women and girls, were recruited to fill shells with the mustard gas produced just up the road. This process was equally hazardous and in less than six months, 1,213 injuries were reported. To counter extremely high sickness and absenteeism rates the hours of work were reduced, and one week's holiday was granted for every 20 days worked. By the standards of the day this would seem an absurdly generous arrangement, but it simply reflected the horrendous nature of the work. Among those injured was a teenage girl, Maud Isaacs, from Barton Hill. She was unfortunate enough to have some mustard gas spill on her feet and according to her grandson, Richard Burley, who works at the Bristol Record Office, the effects of this lasted for the rest of her life, with a vivid yellow discharge regularly erupting through the skin on her feet.

Numerous compensation payments for injured workers were still being agreed two years after the war ended. Most, like Maud Isaacs, received nothing, but because all employees at the factory had signed the Official Secrets Act, very little information came out until some time after the war had ended. It is therefore unarguable that, as far as Avonmouth was concerned, the men fighting at the front were by no means the only ones who suffered real hardship and danger during the First World War. The irony was that these people worked in terrible conditions and risked their lives to little purpose; mustard gas from Avonmouth did not arrive at the front until September 18, 1918, less than two months before Armistice Day. On the other hand, it could be argued that Avonmouth mustard gas probably changed the course of history forever, and for this reason. One night in October 1918 British troops fired some of their gas shells into German positions at a Belgian village named Werwick, and one of the injured, an Austrian-born corporal, wrote later:

How these German soldiers behind the lines drank all that wine while still wearing gas masks is not known

> On the night of October 13, the English gas attack on the southern front before Ypres burst loose. They used yellow-cross gas (the German soldiers' name for mustard gas), whose effects were still unknown to us… On this night I was myself to become acquainted with it. On a hill south of Werwick, gas shells were fired which continued all night more or less violently. As early as midnight, a number of us passed out, a few of our comrades forever. Toward morning I, too, was seized with pain which grew worse with every quarter hour, and at seven in the morning I stumbled and tottered back with burning eyes; taking with me my last report of the war. A few hours later, my eyes had turned into glowing coals; it had grown dark around me.

The corporal was evacuated back to Germany by train, blinded, burned, and desperate for revenge. His name was Adolf Hitler.

34   PAPER BAGS

Made by ES & A Robinson

ELISHA SMITH ROBINSON came originally from the village of Overbury, near Tewkesbury where his father owned a small paper mill. In his school holidays he helped out in his grandfather's shop in the nearby village of Blockley. While working behind the counter he couldn't help but notice that each customer's purchases had to be carefully and laboriously decanted onto a single sheet of paper and then the ends twisted in such a way that the sugar, tea, flour or whatever it was didn't spill out. When he left school young Elisha didn't have much choice when it came to a trade. It had to be something to do with paper. Accordingly he was sent away to serve an apprenticeship before coming back to work in the family firm. But Overbury was a small village and the idea of working in the same family firm for the rest of his life didn't excite him. He decided to leave and come to Bristol to make his own way.

There he decided that there had to be a better way to package groceries and paper bags were the answer. He started his own business in Baldwin Street in 1844 with capital of £190. He worked extremely hard, cleaned his own windows, swept the floor and polished the brass himself. In his first year of business he made a profit of £400. In 1846, less than two years later, he moved to much larger premises in 2, Redcliff Street where he described his business as 'paper merchant and grocer's stationer.' In 1848 his younger brother Alfred also left Overbury and joined the business. Together they became ES & A Robinson, a name you'll still see written large on the side of a redbrick factory building in Bedminster, next to Cameron Balloons. In 1850 the two brothers decided to invest in a hand lithographic press which enabled them to print the grocer's name, illustrations and advertisements on their paper bags and wrapping paper. Six years later they bought a mechanised printing machine to do the same job far more quickly.

Their willingness to invest in new technology didn't stop there. Up till then paper bags had been made in a grotesquely labour-intensive and inefficient way as described in a magazine of the time: 'Printers would purchase a few reams of paper and a bedraggled, worn-looking woman would visit his premises and stagger away with a ream which she would cut by hand into shaped pieces and make into paper bags with which she would wend her weary way back to the printing office so that she might be paid the meagre pittance she had so laboriously earned. Certainly this was not conducive to hygiene for such poor women lived generally in unwholesome rooms.' The Robinson brothers clearly thought this convoluted process should be mechanised and in 1860 introduced a paper-bag making machine.

Their first machine worked well enough but in 1873, after a trip to America, Elisha acquired, in return for a large sum of money, the British rights to a new, far more

E. S. & A. ROBINSON & C⁰.,
BRISTOL.

The original Robinson building on the corner of Redcliff Street and Victoria Street

advanced American bag-making machine. This had been invented by an American woman called Margaret E. Knight, sometimes dubbed 'the mother of the paper bag' or 'the female Edison'. (She had earlier invented a machine for cutting shoe soles, an internal combustion engine and a new kind of sash window.) Her machine automatically folded the paper to create between 100 and 200 flat-bottomed paper bags a minute. It was this machine that really made the Robinson brothers' fortune since, according to a Victorian trade journal, the machine-produced bags which 'when opened, afforded a ready-made bag of rectangular shape, easily filled. The introduction of bags made on this principle completely revolutionised the industry in this country.' What became of the 'bedraggled, worn-looking women' who lost their jobs is not recorded, but that's progress for you.

ES & A Robinson were now very successful and in 1878 had a massive new factory built specially for them in the Bristol Byzantine style on the corner of Redcliff Street and Victoria Street. This building however only lasted 25 years before it was partly destroyed by a disastrous fire.

From paper bags the Robinson brothers branched out into almanacs. In 1882 they

Robinson's paper bag factory in East Street, Bedminster

produced 685,000 annually, all in full colour, the Victorian equivalent of today's pin-up calendars. Hours of work may have been long, but a visitor to the factory remarked in 1883 that 'wherever we went, we noticed that the hands, both male and female, seemed to be of a superior class, and that they are evidently well-satisfied and contented'. The printing side of the business was so successful that yet another new factory had to be built in 1887, this time in Bedminster. Elisha was by this time a pillar of the Bristol community, a staunch Baptist, a Justice of the Peace, a Liberal politician, a supporter of the Avonmouth Dock scheme and eventually Mayor of Bristol. He died in 1885 and his two sons Edward and Arthur took over the business.

Expansion didn't stop there. In 1912 the new Malago Vale factory was opened in Bedminster and was described in fulsome terms by a contemporary magazine:

> It is one of the finest factories in Bristol, covering half an acre of land, with five storeys and with everything in the way of improvement that 70 years of experience could suggest. Here the workers find themselves in light, airy and well-ventilated workrooms with excellent dining-rooms and the flat roof devoted to a playground while the pots of growing flowers on the window sills give an added note of cheerfulness. At this factory many millions of paper bags are turned out every week ranging from that made to hold half an ounce of tea to the giant specimen for the carrying of 28lbs of coke. Yes!

Today, after many reincarnations, E S & A Robinsons has become Rexams, a multinational company formed in 1996, which specialises in medical packaging, in particular blister packs for pills. Rexams is now part of an even bigger multinational, Amcor. The company has eight factories in or near Bristol. Their new factory in Stoke Gifford has a production area of 7,000 square metres or, put another way, six football pitches – a far cry from Elisha Robinson's small grocer's shop in Baldwin Street.

Made by Clark's Pies and Pieminister

CLARK'S PIES ARE FOR MANY BRISTOLIANS an institution, but their story started in Cardiff a hundred years ago. There, Mary Clark, a young widow and mother of nine children, was working as a housekeeper and cook for a wealthy family. Once a week she made them one of her steak and kidney pies in a big dish. One day she broke the dish and had to make individual pies instead. These reputedly tasted so good that her family suggested she should make a few extra at home and sell them to neighbours.

Eventually she put up a table on the pavement outside her terrace house and sold them to passers-by. This was the start of Clark's Pies.

Roger Clark

Soon after that, Mary's son Percy persuaded her to rent a small shop nearby, and Clark's pies are still made and sold in Cardiff by a different branch of the family. Percy, however, decided to move to the other side of the Bristol Channel, and in 1929 he started up his own business in Church Road, Redfield, making pies using his mother's tried-and-tested but still secret recipe. Then, in 1935, he was in Bedminster when he noticed hundreds of women and girls streaming out of the Wills cigarette factory on North Street, many of them wanting to buy something to eat and queuing outside a baker's shop. He calculated that a shop in Bedminster, with so many potential customers, could sell many more pies than in Redfield, and bought the baker's shop at 259, North Street, which had a large coke-fired oven at the back. He, his wife Nellie Louisa and his four children promptly moved in and lived over the shop.

During the Second World War, Percy would be on fire watch on the roof while Nellie Louisa baked 'Aunt Nellie's Veggie Pies' below, with vegetables grown on Percy's allotment because meat was strictly rationed. Their eldest son John started working for the business when he was 15 and stayed for the next 42 years – reluctantly at first, because he had the idea that he wanted to be an astronomer rather than a pieman. He tells a story illustrating how important Clark's pies are to many Bristolians. His father Percy was serving in the shop one day in 1946 when a soldier who had just been demobbed came in. He said he had been fighting in Burma for the last four years and had often dreamed of coming home and eating a Clark's pie. Then, with his dream come true, he licked his lips and left the shop to be finally reunited with his wife and family. Percy thought he had his priorities right, although the homecoming hero's wife might not have agreed.

In 1989 John Clark retired and his younger brother Ken took over the business. He in turn handed over to his younger brother Roger until 2007 when, to make it four generations of the Clark family, his daughter Dawn took over, together with her partner Keith Prested. Neither of them was an experienced pie maker; both had been ballet

Keith Prested in front of the Clark's pies shop and bakery in North Street

dancers with the Scottish Ballet and Keith's only knowledge of pies came from selling them at a Wimpy Bar in Glasgow. But they learned fast and the family business is still thriving. They employ eight women and six men making the famous pies and four or five drivers to deliver them. There is no age limit or fixed retirement age. One Clark's employee, Buster Devonport, is 76. The meat in the pies is good quality beef to which is added ox kidneys, onions, potatoes, herbs, salt, pepper, seasoning, and most important of all, that special gravy. The pastry is thick enough not to need a foil tray. They bake the pies 200 at a time and make on average 2,000 a day. In a hot summer that number goes right down. A cold winter pushes it right up again. They are best eaten straight out of the oven, though regular customers have learned to beware of a 'Clark's tash', the result of burning the upper lip with the hot filling. Clark's also make a steak and ale pie with beer, or Red Ale to be exact, direct from the Bristol Beer Factory just down the road. They also make a few hundred pasties which they call 'short crust', because to call them Cornish would be stretching the truth by a hundred miles or so. They start work at 6.30 in the morning, so Clark's are telling the truth when they say 'freshly baked every day'. Eight out of ten of their products are delivered daily to about 200 outlets – fish-and-chip shops, pubs, corner shops and sports grounds. But many people buy direct from the shop on North Street, where one of their regulars confirmed the pie's status as a Bristol institution: 'Clark's pies is just Bristol, isn't it? I've come here for years. It's good old-fashioned grub, and that's the way I like it!'

Clark's pies just out of the oven

It is a prodigous leap from Clark's traditional pies to the zappy world of Pieministcr. Their all-singing, all-dancing website will give you the idea: 'Welcome to the steamy, tasty, lovely world of Pieminister. Enjoy. XX.' It then goes on: 'Free-range chirpy chickens, carefree cows, smiley sheep and perky pigs help us make our lovely food. Yum yum, put a pie in your tum.'

Pieminister started relatively recently when Jon Simon and his brother-in-law Tristan Hogg got together to start a pie business. They say with considerable chutzpah that 'they wanted to offer the great British public what they really deserved – a really good pie made from proper stuff.' Tristan had been working as a chef, cooking for rock stars on tour all over the world and Jon had been running a gastro-pub in London. Together they developed the recipe for their first gourmet pie in a basement in Bristol and in June 2003 launched their product on an unsuspecting public. The catchy name probably helped but the quality of their pies ensured they continued to sell. Nowadays Pieminister sell as many as 70,000 pies a week to restaurants, bars, pubs and delis all over the country, not to mention up to 60 music festivals a year. They also supply big supermarkets such as Sainsbury's and Waitrose as well as their own shops and market stalls. Their turnover in 2010 was more than £7 million – not bad for a specialist company less than 10 years old. So why are they so popular? Says Jon:

> It all comes from the ingredients. If you start with good-quality, free-range British meat and fresh vegetables, you don't want to spoil it by putting in lots of additives and preservatives and hydrogenated fats.

The founders of Pieminister, Jon Simon and his brother-in-law Tristan Hogg

Their pies come in an almost bewildering variety of flavours. How about these two: 'wildshroom and asparagus pie – wild mushrooms, asparagus, shallots, white wine and cracked black pepper in lovely pastry' and 'chicken of arragon pie – free-range British chicken, smoky bacon, roast garlic, vermouth and fresh tarragon'. So why are Pieminister here in Bristol? According to Simon:

> We started in Bristol because it's a green-minded city, with lots of students and people who would rather eat a locally-reared chicken than one that's been flown in from Peru with thousands of food miles attached. In the process, though, we've discovered that people all over the country have this obsessive, rather perfectionist attitude towards pies. They absolutely love a good one and they hate a bad one with surprising intensity. Maybe it's something to do with childhood memories, or comfort-eating, but pies seem to stir up strong emotions.

That is doubtless a sentiment Clark's Pies would wholeheartedly agree with.

PILOT CUTTERS

36

Made by RB Boatbuilding and Bristol Classic Boat Company

TO UNDERSTAND THE ROLE of pilots and pilot cutters you have to understand Bristol's position as a major port. During the eighteenth and nineteenth centuries Britain, with its empire and connections with the West Indies and North America, was the busiest trading nation in the world, and Bristol, on the west coast and facing the Atlantic, was ideally placed to take advantage. Apart from that though, the city did not have much going for it as a port. For a start it was six miles inland up the winding Avon Gorge which meant that it could sometimes take more than two days for a ship to be towed upstream from the mouth of the river Avon to the port of Bristol. This was slow, labour-intensive work done originally by 'hobblers'. These were teams of strong men, and sometimes women, who unbelievably sometimes pulled big ships, or at least guided them with the incoming tide, upstream into port. Other teams of hobblers towed them behind a small 'fleet' of rowing boats. Big ships sometimes needed as many as fifty oarsmen in five or more boats.

Another problem was that the river was extremely tidal; in fact the Severn estuary at the mouth of the Avon has the second-highest tidal range in the world of up to 14.5 metres. This meant that the twists and turns of the river went from one extreme to the other, with steep muddy banks at low tide and only a narrow navigable channel at high tide. Even when they finally reached the port, ships moored at St Augustine's Reach, where the city centre is today, spent a lot of time on the mud until the great Floating Harbour project, bringing stable water levels to the docks, solved the problem in 1810. It did nothing to improve the river, however, and as ships grew increasingly bigger as the nineteenth century progressed, it was not surprising that their masters turned to the much safer and less expensive port of Liverpool.

As if all this was not bad enough, there was also the formidable problem of the Bristol Channel, a notoriously difficult estuary to navigate with extreme tidal differences, strong currents, rocky shores and shifting mud banks. This is where the Bristol pilots came in. Ship owners and merchants were clearly not going to risk their vessels or their cargoes on the first or final leg of their voyage, so hiring the services of a pilot was essential. Most other port authorities employed these men, but Bristol pilots were different. They were fiercely independent characters who worked on an every-man-for himself basis. They operated a form of closed shop – jobs were normally passed on from father to son: the pilot responsible for taking John Cabot's ship the *Matthew* safely out to sea en route to north America in 1497 was George James Ray, while in 1837 George Ray, from the same Pill family, was the pilot on board the ss *Great Western* on her maiden voyage. Seven years later William Ray piloted the ss *Great Britain*

Morwenna at
Underfall Yard

out of Bristol in 1844. The central role of the village of Pill, three miles downstream from the city, is confirmed by the 1830 edition of *Pigot's Directory of Bristol*, which listed 27 pilots living there. By 1863 the number had increased to 74.

These pilots had to look for work; it did not come to them. This meant pilot cutters sailed out westwards with the pilot and two men on board, the skipper or 'westerman' and his apprentice. They sometimes went out more than 100 miles, beyond Land's End or the south coast of Ireland, in search of an incoming merchant ship, and there they sometimes had to wait for a week or more, hove to, just waiting and hoping, however bad the weather. It rewarded the most adventurous (and luckiest) pilots handsomely, because ship owners and merchants were prepared to pay very well for their services; before the days of accurate, detailed charts or modern navigational aids it was a small price for the safety of a ship and its cargo. Having hailed a ship, the pilot traditionally changed clothes into a formal suit with a bow tie and fob watch, and a small clinker-built rowing boat (or 'punt') was launched. The apprentice then rowed him from the cutter to the ship, leaving the westerman aboard, and in heavy seas this called for extremely high levels of seamanship. The pilot then did his job taking the merchant vessel up into Bristol, or in some cases Cardiff, Newport and Barry, while the westerman followed him into port and then took him home to Pill.

As for the boats that carried these pilots, the Bristol cutters, many experts say they were the pinnacle of boat design in combining form and function; their design evolved to meet exactly the demands of the pilots who owned them. They were usually between 40 to 60 feet long with a deep hull, a long keel and a heavy displacement. Below decks they could accommodate two or three men in reasonable comfort, while up above

John Raymond-Barker at
Underfall Yard with the
replica cutter *Mischief* on
the water behind

they had a powerful gaff cutter rig with a sturdy central mast, a gaff main sail, a top sail and two smaller head sails. To do their job they had to be fast, manoeuvrable but rugged. Of the hundreds of original Bristol cutters, only about 18 survive today. They became redundant after the First World War, when steam cutters superseded them. But because they are arguably so beautiful and well designed, a local industry has sprung up building modern-day cutters which are all but exact replicas of the originals.

The most famous of these makers is RB Boatbuilding in the Underfall Yard, fittingly close to where the Floating Harbour ends and exits into the river Avon. RB stands for (John) Raymond-Barker, the man who started the business. He came from Rye, where fishing boats and sailing ships are still pulled up on the shingle beach, and as an agricultural engineer he worked for Médicins Sans Frontières for some time. He has always loved boats and sailing, however, and in 2002 he decided to start this venture in Bristol. It took five men three years to build his first Bristol cutter, *Mischief*, working part-time. John's boats usually have six-ton lead keels supplemented by another six to ten tons of ballast. The wooden part of the keel is made from purple-heart, a South American hardwood, the frame of the boat from European oak and the planking from Scottish larch, which is rot-resistant and long-lasting. The leftovers or offcuts are then used for fitting out down below; some customers could ask for some-

Mark Rolt of the
Bristol Classic Boat
Company in his
boatyard on
Redcliffe Quay

thing fancier, like mahogany or teak, although RB Boatbuilding emphasise that they build a converted working boat rather than a gentleman's yacht. The whole boat is then held together with specially made bronze nails, screws and bolts from the Bristol Foundry at Brislington. Sails might look and feel like traditional canvas, but are made of a synthetic modern equivalent which does not rot. Similarly, ropes are not made from traditional hemp but from a polypropylene material which looks remarkably like it but is far stronger and lasts much longer. There are other concessions to the twenty-first century. These cutters might look traditional from the outside but down below they are spacious and comfortable; five could sleep there in comfort, eight at a push.

Four or five men are employed more or less full-time building Bristol cutters, one at a time, each one taking approximately 18 months. They do the job because they love it, not because they earn a lot. Many of them also love sailing, and are never happier than when they are out on the boats they helped build. When sailing, because of its solid construction a Bristol cutter ploughs a furrow rather than bobs about like a cork or a plastic boat of the same size; it is down in the water, not on top of it. This also helps give it an easy motion, especially in heavy seas, which is far less likely to make you seasick. This, though, is just a small part of the attraction; because of the way they are hand-made by real craftsmen, the boats look right, sound right, smell right and feel right. They are like classic cars, and thankfully there are enough people out there who would prefer to drive around in a Bentley or Jaguar E Type rather than a modern tin box, people who would probably share the sentiments of Ben Punter, one of the young men who works at R B Boatbuilding: 'Boat design has gone backwards since the days of the Bristol cutter.'

So how much does a modern Bristol cutter cost? You wouldn't get much change from £300,000 but interestingly enough you'd have to pay considerably more for a modern plastic equivalent of the same size. And £300,000 is a small price to pay for a superb example of the boat-builders craft and a living piece of Bristol's maritime history.

In the interests of fairness another boatbuilder, the Bristol Classic Boat Company, should also be mentioned since they were responsible for building a very fine 56-foot Bristol pilot cutter named *Pegasus* which was launched by broadcaster and keen sailor, Libby Purves in May 2008. The Rolt brothers, Mark and Peter, who own the yard on Redcliffe Wharf, in the shadow of St Mary Redcliffe church, assembled a team of dedicated boatbuilders who spent thousands of man hours building the classic pilot cutter for the Island Trust, a charity which offers sailing to disadvantaged young people. The Rolt brothers, like John Raymond-Barker, passionately believe that when it comes to boats, 'wood is good'.

37

PRIVATE AIRLINER (BRITAIN FIRST)

Made by the Bristol Aeroplane Company

IN 1933 LORD ROTHERMERE, the proprietor of the *Daily Mail* and at the time supporter of the British Union of Fascists, had what was probably an alcohol-fuelled editorial lunch during which the conversation turned to aeroplanes. One of his editors later wrote:

> Rothermere complained about the amount of delay there was getting a plane into the air from the drawing board stage. All the experts came down to the factory from the Air Ministry demanding modifications to suit their own particular field, with the result that a plane that was three years ahead at its design stage was three years behind in achievement when it got into the air. In fact we were all engaged in producing the obsolete.

To remedy this Rothermere announced: 'I shall have a plane built that will be the fastest commercial aeroplane in Europe, if not the world, and it will be built in one year from the order.'

The newspaper proprietor had long been interested in air travel – he was president of the Air Council for a time during the First World War – and had recently visited the USA, where he had seen a Douglas DC1, the plane which later evolved into the famous DC3 Dakota. He was impressed by this new medium-sized aircraft which could carry 12 passengers at what was then the very high speed of 190 mph, and in a rash moment he announced that he was prepared to offer a prize of £100,000 to the makers of a similar but faster British plane which must also be the fastest in Europe. He reasoned that it would be good for Britain, good for the British aviation industry and probably above all, good for the sales of his newspaper.

It just so happened that the chief designer at the Bristol Aeroplane Company, a Scot called Frank Barnwell, had already sketched out plans for a commercial aircraft of exactly the type of executive express that Lord Rothermere and exceedingly rich people like him might buy. He called it the Type 135, and with the sizeable incentive of a cheque for £100,000, he did further work on his plans for what was a quite radical new aircraft, an all-metal monocoque monoplane with two radial engines and sufficient room for six passengers and two crew. One of its most significant design features was its very low wing position, which theoretically maximised the plane's speed potential. As for the twin engines, the company's chief engine designer, Roy Fedden, had come up with a new six-cylinder radial engine producing 500 hp which he dubbed the Aquilia – but at the time it had never been installed in an aircraft.

"Britain First" Bristol Type 142

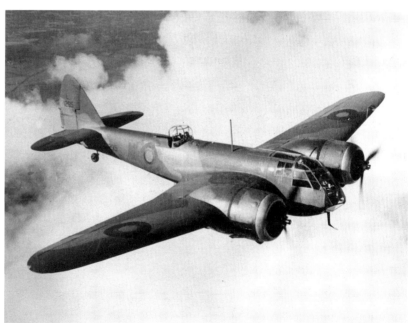

The Bristol Blenheim, the bomber ordered by the RAF, was the military version of Britain First

It was at this point that the editor of the Rothermere-owned *Bristol Evening World*, Robert Lewis, stepped in. He had been at a lecture given by Roy Fedden in March 1934 at the Grand Spa Hotel in Clifton, at which the Type 135 was mentioned. He contacted his boss Rothermere and told him that, on the drawing board at least, a plane to suit his criteria already existed. Negotiations involving the magnate, the aircraft designer and the engine designer, with Lewis acting as a go-between, resulted on March 26, 1934 with the announcement that Rothermere had ordered a single Type 135. Later that month it was disclosed that he was prepared to pay £18,500 for the completed aircraft.

Construction of two prototypes was started. Rothermere's aircraft was to be fitted with two 650hp Mercury engines. The other slightly different prototype with Aquilia engines could accommodate eight passengers. The first flight took place on April 12, 1935 from Filton, and Rothermere, with typical flag-waving patriotism, named the new aircraft Britain First, although Bristol preferred to call it the Type 142. Everyone was highly pleased with its performance, especially when the test pilot demonstrated that it could cruise at over 250 mph and it had a sensational top speed of 307mph. (To put this in context, the RAF's fastest fighter at the time, a biplane by the name of the Gloster Gladiator, was flat out at 220 mph, and a newly designed bomber, the Boulton Paul Overstrand, struggled to reach 148 mph.) Rothermere, doubtless with an eye on the favourable publicity, promptly donated his new aircraft to the Air Ministry. Britain First cost his lordship the huge sum of £18,500 plus the £100,000 prize money – but he could afford it. Unfortunately, an Air Ministry pilot promptly managed to crash-land the prototype. and the ministry paid Lord Rothermere £18,500 to cover its embarrassment.

In 1935 Britain First re-emerged from the factory at Filton as the Bristol Blenheim bomber, of which a total of 5,500 were built. But that was a slightly different aircraft and another story.

Made by H W Carter

H W Carter and Company, a small firm in Ashton Gate near the Bristol City football ground, had been making drinks based on citrus fruits since 1872. But in the late 1930s, with the Second World War looming, there was a real risk that supplies of oranges and lemons would be cut off by German U boats in the Atlantic. Carter's contacted the Long Ashton Research Station and asked them to come up with an alternative non-citrus fruit which they could use in their drinks. The scientists there, led by Dr Vernon Charley, produced a concentrated blackcurrant juice which Mr Lennox at Carter's called Ribena, from the Latin botanical name for blackcurrant, *Ribes nigrum*. The drink was first launched in 1938.

The new drink was approved by the government because its contents were entirely home-grown and contained very high concentrations of vitamin C, five times as much as in orange juice. Initially it was sold on a relatively small scale to hospitals and maternity homes, but then Carter's made the decision to equip a new factory for the large-scale production of fruit syrups, in particular blackcurrant juice. It proved a smart move. During the war, it was deemed so important to the health of the nation's babies and young children that blackcurrant juice was given to them free, and the company prospered. After the war the idea that blackcurrant juice, and Ribena in particular, was good for children's health was fixed very firmly in the nation's subconscious. Unfortunately, Carter's factory had been

damaged by German bombing and the firm could not cope with the huge demand for its product. At the same time, the government offered the company big financial incentives to move out to the Forest of Dean, where there was severe unemployment following the closure of many of its coal mines. As a result, in 1947 it moved its manufacturing base to Coleford. Eight years later, the Ribena brand was bought from Carter's by Beechams, which metamorphosed into the giant multinational GlaxoSmithKline in 1989. It now produces 750 million bottles and cartons of Ribena a year, and the company reckons it uses 95 per cent of all the blackcurrants grown in Britain – 13,600 tonnes or 19 billion currants a year, give or take a few. Nowadays it is supplied by 40 or so large-scale growers, including the Queen's farm at Sandringham.

Ribena might be more expensive than the dozens of fruit-flavoured fizzy drinks on supermarket shelves, but it continues to sell in vast quantities in more than 20 countries all over the world. GlaxoSmithKline, however, have had one or two problems with their product. In New Zealand in 2007, two 14-year-old schoolgirls decided to test Ribena's claim that it contained four times the vitamin C of oranges. In a simple experiment they found only minute quantities of vitamin C, and as a result a court found the company guilty of 15 breaches of the Fair Trading Act and fined it NZ$217,400. GlaxoSmithKline paid the fine and, probably through clenched teeth, wrote to the girls thanking them for 'bringing the matter to our attention'.

In Britain at least, Ribena is still advertised using echoes of its origins with slogans like 'Rich in memories, rich in vitamin C' – and people of a certain age write to the company with comments like

> Ribena for me brings back memories of childhood, especially when you had a cold and you were in bed shivering. The welcome smell of Ribena as your mum entered your bedroom with a hot cup of the stuff already made you feel much better.

Ribena's connections with Bristol have long since been severed, but should not be forgotten.

Made by Douglas under licence from Vespa

SOME PEOPLE OF A CERTAIN AGE get misty-eyed when they hear the names Matchless, Norton, AJS, Royal Enfield, Triumph, BSA and Douglas. Today only Norton and Triumph survive, but there was a time, particularly in the 1930s and '40s, when these very British motorcycles dominated the world markets. It did not last. Japanese motorbikes began to dominate in the 1960s, and the British industry went into terminal decline.

This demise affected the Bristol firm of Douglas as much as any. Production of their motorcycles had slumped, and in 1948 the company was bankrupt and officially in receivership. Perhaps in desperation, the flamboyant managing director, Claude McCormack, went off on holiday to Italy, where he could not help but notice the popularity of a new-fangled form of transport, the Vespa. The Italian firm of Piaggio had made fighter aircraft during the Second World War, but their Pontedera factory had been flattened by Allied bombs. After the war, under the terms of the armistice, the company was prohibited from making planes, so their chief aircraft designer came up instead with a vehicle that reflected the fact that petrol was expensive and the vast majority of Italians could not afford a car.

The Road to happiness...

It was the scooter, and it was radically different. It had a curvy monocoque body which completely covered the engine over the rear wheel, a platform to rest your feet on and a leg shield to protect you from the wind and rain. Significantly, unlike motorcycles, it had no dirty, oily chain. When he first saw it and heard the sound of its engine, Enrico Piaggio laughed: 'Sembra una vespa!' (It's like a wasp!) The name stuck. In 1946 the company cleverly introduced it to the Italian press at the very smart Rome Golf Club. It was clearly intended to be used by style-conscious young Italians, particularly women, because its step-through design meant it could easily be ridden by anyone wearing the then fashionable pencil skirts, with their knees together. (A woman wearing a skirt on a motorbike is somewhat less than elegant.) From the start, Piaggio pushed the Vespa brand for all it was worth. The marketing was as brilliant as the design. The Vespa was an instant success, and two years later the Piaggio factory was producing 20,000 a year; by 1950 this had increased to 60,000. Then, in 1952, Piaggio pulled off an outrageous piece of product placement. In the popular film of that year, *Roman Holiday*, Gregory Peck was repeatedly shown riding round the streets of Rome with the beautiful Audrey Hepburn riding sidesaddle behind him – on a Vespa! With free publicity like this, it was no surprise that by 1956 they had sold a million Vespas and the Italian government declared April 16 a public holiday, Vespa Day. Fifteen cities all over Italy had festivals to mark the occasion.

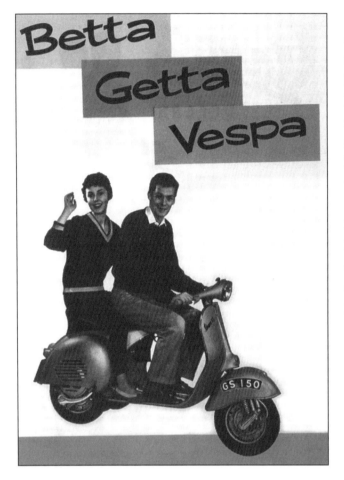

Back at the Douglas factory, Claude McCormack concluded that conditions in post-war Britain were similar to those in Italy, and the scooter might become just as popular. He contacted Enrico Piaggio and sold him the idea of Douglas making and selling Vespas for him in Britain and most of the Commonwealth countries. He clearly did a good selling job – with his trademark cigars and shiny Rolls Royce, he was obviously a polished salesman – and in 1950 the two companies signed a contract.

The first Vespa GL was made in Bristol in March 1951. It had a 125cc engine and cost £117. 5s (plus purchase tax). It had the same Italian metallic green paintwork and most of the parts were imported, but some, like the Lucas electrics, Amal carburettors and seats and tyres, were made in Britain. Which first meant that the Douglas factory was more than simply an assembly plant and besides, the Douglas Vespa had a distinguishing feature – because of some obscure British regulation, the headlight had to be moved from the handlebars to the front mudguard. When scooters became a compulsory fashion item for Mods in the early 1960s, production in Kingswood was stepped up to 125 a week. Sales were further helped by the Irish police buying a large quantity for their men on the beat. But production never reached the levels Claude McCormack had promised and Piaggio expected, as is clear in this terse letter (translated from the Italian) from the parent company:

I gather that production from April to July has practically remained unchanged, with a monthly total of little more than 300 Vespa scooters. You will be kind enough to consider e.g. that monthly consignments of more than 1,000 Vespas are made by us to the Swiss market alone, and you will easily understand why I consider the quantity of your production completely inadequate.

Things went from bad to worse, and a year later Enrico Piaggio wrote another letter:

Vespa 125

A Douglas Vespa plus sidecar, on display at the Kingswood Heritage Museum

A very young-looking Cliff Richard on the back of a Douglas Vespa

> If you consider the immensity of the territory we have granted Douglas to exploit exclusively, and you compare it with the poor production programmes, you have to agree that this contract was bad business for my company.

The message is clear: Piaggio were seriously regretting their decision to get involved with Douglas, especially since Lambrettas, their great competitors, were easily outselling Vespas on the UK market. Production continued in a half-hearted sort of way until 1965, by which time a total of 126,230 Douglas Vespas had been made. Then Piaggio finally gave up on their Bristol collaborators, and the factory closed for good two years later. Meanwhile, more than 50 million Vespas have been sold worldwide.

40 SHERRY

Made by Harvey's

BRISTOL HAS A CONNECTION with wine and sherry that goes back as far as the twelfth century, when Henry Plantagenet married Eleanor of Aquitaine. When, two years later, he became Henry II of England, the doors were opened to the large-scale importation of French wine, in particular from Gascony in the south-west, which was then an English possession. The first record of French wine coming into Bristol was in 1180. Most of the French wine of the south west region was exported via Bordeaux, and Bristol was an obvious first port of call. By the beginning of the fourteenth century 756,000 gallons of French wine had been unloaded on Bristol docks. When Gascony reverted to being French, the wine merchants of Bristol looked for other sources of supply. Spain and Portugal were obvious candidates and by the sixteenth century a third of the wine shipped into Bristol was Spanish, including a fortified wine from the south west called sherry, a corruption of Jerez, the region's name. Vaults to store the wine were dug beneath the streets, and they are still there today. In fact the condition of these wines was judged to be so important that wheeled vehicles were banned from certain streets, and only sledges pulled by dogs were allowed, so that the vaults were not disturbed.

The Harvey family's connection with the wine trade started early in the nineteenth century when John Harvey married into a family that had a business importing and selling sherry and port from premises in Denmark Street. These made use of cellars that were originally part of a thirteenth-century Augustinian monastery based in and around what is now Bristol Cathedral. John Harvey eventually took over the firm and when his sons joined, it became John Harvey and Sons Limited in 1871.

The name Bristol Cream goes back far further. In 1634, a visitor to Bristol wrote that 'with a cup of Bristow milk, we parted with our honest and grave host and bad this sweet city adieu'. Similarly, Samuel Pepys recorded in his diary in 1668 that his maid's father:

> did give us good entertainment of strawberries, a whole venison pasty and plenty of brave wine, and above all Bristol Milk.

So it seems that as early as the seventeenth century there was such a drink as Bristol Milk, and one writer at the time hazarded that 'some will have called it Milk because such wine is the first moisture given infants in the city'. Fanciful, of course, but Bristol and sherry were clearly closely connected even then. As for Bristol Cream, the story goes that in 1882, John Harvey and Sons were experimenting with various blends and

one day, a French woman at a sherry tasting in Denmark Street said 'If that was the milk, then this must be the cream!' John Harvey duly registered it as the company's trademark, and in 1901, when the Prince of Wales visited the city, he murmured: 'Bristol must have damn fine cows!'

The firm expanded and prospered and in 1908 it started to advertise its products instead of relying simply on word of mouth. An export trade to the USA followed, and during the First World War the company worked hard supplying the officers' messes of the army and navy, as well as military hospitals, where red burgundy or claret were thought to speed recovery. Mechanical bottling and automatic labelling machines were brought in in 1919, and the company continued to expand until one

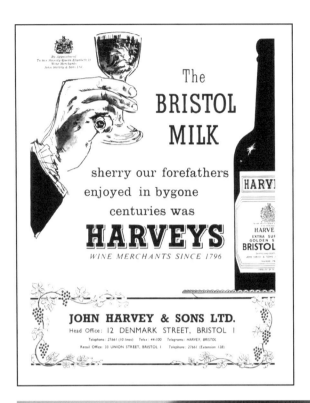

night in November 1940 when its premises received a direct hit in the Bristol blitz. The office, warehouse, thousands of bottles of fine wines and sherries and all the company's records were completely destroyed, and only the cellars were left. The firm somehow survived, however, and in 1958 it moved out to new, purpose-built premises in Whitchurch, which cost £500,000. There as many as 3,550 dozen bottles an hour could be filled, most of them to be exported to 114 different countries. In 1966 Harvey's were taken over by Showerings of Shepton Mallet, and the family's links with the firm were finally lost. Showerings were in turn taken over by Allied Breweries and then the multinational Allied Domecq, which resulted in the production of Bristol Milk and Bristol Cream being moved to Spain. Even the famous Harvey's restaurant, in the cellars of the firm's original headquarters, was closed in 2003. Finally, the Allied Domeq offices next to the Bedminster Down crematorium closed and the company was taken over by the huge conglomerate Pernod Ricard in 2005.

Importantly, though, you can still drink Bristol Cream. The grapes are grown in enormous 2,000-acre company-owned vineyards in the Jerez region, and the sherry is left to age in 500-gallon oak casks for eight years before it is bottled and sold. As it has an alcohol content of 17.5 per cent, it should be sipped, rather than drunk. According to one wine critic, it has 'smoky orange rind and caramel aromas with the flavour of vanilla bean, toasted caramel and toffee'. Whatever, it tastes good, and while Harvey's Bristol Milk and Bristol Cream might not be produced here any longer, its association with Bristol lives on on the label of every bottle.

Made by Charles Hill & Sons

HILHOUSE WAS A LONG-ESTABLISHED FIRM of Bristol shipbuilders which had started shipbuilding in the 1740s and expanded rapidly when it won an Admiralty contract to build warships for the American War of Independence, 1000-ton ships each with 50 guns. When peace resumed the company switched to merchant ships for the West India run and profited from the last years of the slave trade. In 1810, an 18-year old junior accountant named Charles Hill joined the firm. In 1820 the company bought 10 acres of unused land opposite Hotwells and built two wet docks, a dry dock and several slipways on the south side of the floating harbour (near where the ss *Great Britain* is now). At the same time they built an impressive Regency villa for the up-and-coming Charles Hill next to his shipyard. By 1825 Charles Hill was made a partner and in 1839 the company was renamed Hilhouse, Hill & Company. But Charles Hill's ambition still wasn't satisfied and he subsequently took over the whole business when Hilhouse died.

In 1845, to reinforce his family's control, he brought his 16-year-old son into the business (a boy who predictably had been given the same name as his father). The firm was subsequently renamed Charles Hill & Sons. Three years later their New Dockyard was renamed the Albion Dockyard. In 1854 the widower Charles Hill re-married and to mark the occasion some of his workforce resurrected a rusty old cannon they found lying around the shipyard and attempted to fire it. Unfortunately it exploded instead, severely injuring Charles Hill's well-wishers.

The problem with shipbuilding in the floating harbour is the narrowness of the harbour. Newly-built ships had to be launched with extreme care to ensure they didn't hit the wall opposite. This was a major factor in Charles Hill's decision to concentrate on building relatively small vessels of 300 to 400 tons. Typical of these was a gunboat named the *Hardy* built in 1856 to aid and abet the government's diplomatic efforts of the time. The *Illustrated London News* even sent a reporter down to witness its launching and, on March 29 1856, he brought the relatively small Bristol shipbuilders to the attention of its national readership.

> Messrs Charles Hill and Sons have lately contracted with the Admiralty for three gun-vessels which they are building under very large sheds which are lighted in every direction with gas thus enabling their people to work at night and day ever since the receipt of the order and besides this advantage their operations are not impeded by rain, and the vessels are rendered more durable, being built

Charles Hill's shipyard viewed from Cliftonwood in 1938. The ship in the centre of the picture is HMS *Barrier*, a boom defence vessel, launched on 17 May, 1938

in the dry. We understand that the authorities are much pleased with the remarkably fine quality of the timbers and plank of the Hardy as also with the workmanship. So smoothly have her sides been finished that it is difficult to distinguish them from iron.

With free publicity like that the orders, not surprisingly, kept coming in. In fact Charles Hill & Sons didn't build its first steel ship until 1881 and its last sailing ship, the *Favell*, in 1895.

Charles Hill senior died in 1866 and his son in 1900 but the company with their name carried on building barges, dredgers, tugs and small tankers. (One of these barges, which is still very much afloat and working after a fashion, is the so-called *Glass Boat*. This was built in 1924 by Charles Hill and started life as a barge carrying bulk timbers up and down the Severn estuary. When its working days were over, it ended up as a tidal breakwater, half submerged in Severn mud until it was rescued, moored and refitted in 1984. It's now one of Bristol's landmark restaurants, moored by Bristol Bridge, barely a mile upstream from where it was built.)

It was during the Second World War that Charles Hill's shipbuilding yards were at their busiest. The yard was badly bombed three times but somehow managed to keep working and between 1938 and 1946 it built eight corvettes and seven frigates as well as well as numerous other smaller ships such as D-Day landing craft. In 1944, in recognition of the company's contribution to the war effort, Queen Mary paid a morale-boosting visit to the shipyard, coming from Badminton where she

spent most of the war years. When the war ended, Hill's employed 1,350 men and 60 women.

After the war Hills switched from warships back to vessels like the paddle steamer the *Bristol Queen*, a lightship, a Scilly Islands ferry and a sand dredger, the *Harry Brown*, which was to become the last ship of any size to use the Bristol Docks as a working port.

But then the orders started to dry up and in 1970, when the forthcoming closure of Bristol City Docks for commercial operations was announced, the writing was on the wall for Charles Hill & Sons. On 9 July, 1976, they launched the last ship ever to be built by the company, the 1,541 ton *Miranda Guinness*, designed to bring vast quantities of Guinness from Dublin to Bristol. It was the end of an era and practically the end of one of Bristol's most important industries.

Postscript: Happily shipbuilding, or rather boatbuilding, has now returned to Bristol, see the entry on pilot Cutters, page 119.

On 9 July 1976 the last ship was launched from Charles Hill shipyard – the *Miranda Guinness*

42 STEAK, CHIPS AND SHERRY

Made by Berni Inns

Frank Berni

IN THE MID-1950s the Rummer was one of many city centre pubs that were historic and atmospheric but also tired and tatty. For some reason it was owned by Bristol Corporation, although not for much longer. When the council decided to give up their job as pub landlords and put it up for sale, the Italian brothers Frank, Marco and Aldo Berni put in an offer. With the help of an interior designer they transformed the Rummer, reputedly one of the oldest pubs in the country, into the first Berni Inn. According to the *Evening Post*:

> In three short weeks a complete transformation has been effected. Thirteen coats of old paint, nearly half an inch thick, had to be removed before the redecoration could begin.

It was the start of something very big. But to go back to the beginning, in the early 1900s after leaving school in the Italian village of Bardi in the Apennines, the Berni brothers said goodbye to their mother and Italy and joined their father in the Welsh valleys. He had a chain of cafés, or 'refreshment bars' as he called them, serving sodas, squash, ice-cream and cigarettes, and they did well until the outbreak of the First World War, when many Welsh Italians were called home to fight. After the war the Depression finally put an end to the chain of 48 cafés, and the brothers moved to Bristol. Unfortunately for them, Italians were not particularly popular in the Second World War, compounded by the fact that Marco had been a member of the Fascist party in Cardiff, and two of the three were interned. The third, Aldo, managed to avoid the same fate, and rejected for military service on medical grounds, he set up a chain of six unlicensed cafés while moonlighting from his job growing vegetables in a market garden. Some of these cafés suffered bomb damage and the money he received from war reparations, together with an inheritance from their mother back in Italy, enabled the brothers to buy a smart and long established restaurant called Horts in 1948. On three floors in Broad Street in the heart of town, it specialised in oyster soup and Dover sole.

In 1954 the opening of the first Berni Inn in the nearby Rummer marked the start of a revolution that changed the eating-out habits of a whole generation of Bristolians, and indeed Britons. 'A Berni' came to be as familiar in the late 1960s as 'a Chinese' at about the same time or 'an Indian' some years later. The phenomenon was the direct result of the ending of meat rationing in 1954 when, for the first time in more than 15 years, the British could gorge themselves on as much meat as they could afford. The

An early Berni, this one a café and ice cream parlour in Wales

Berni formula was simple: a 7s 6d (37.5p) fixed menu included an eight-ounce Argentinian rump steak (bought in, frozen), put on a grill for a few minutes and served with chips and peas, and a bread roll and butter. Portions were strictly controlled – some say even the peas were counted – an idea the brothers had learned from the Americans. The cooking method was so straightforward and idiot-proof that no expensive, tantrum-throwing chef was necessary. Add bought-in exotic starters like prawn cocktails and desserts like Black Forest Gateaux and the menu was complete. To make the formula even more classy, Berni Inns also offered as an aperitif – how posh was that? – schooners of sherry. The term 'schooner' was suggested by Reg Morley, who worked for Gonzales Sherry; the word 'glass' was clearly too ordinary, and besides, these were massive glasses, or so they seemed at the time. The Bernis saw it as a good marketing device, especially when the price of a schooner was only 1s 6d (7p), and within three months they were selling 100 gallons of it a week.

Another reason for Berni Inns' success was timing. In the 1960s eating out became a new mass leisure activity for the first time, and the Bernis were in a strong position to cash in. The other winning element of the formula was to kit their restaurants out like traditional British pubs, hence the word 'inn'. Their designers were briefed to preserve as many traditional features as possible and add a few more of their own; the house style was low ceilings, rich red carpets, plush red banquettes, old prints and

Marco's Italian restaurant just off Baldwin Street, started by the third Berni brother

assorted paraphernalia. Bernis knew very soon that they were on to a winner. They expanded in Bristol and in rapid succession bought a number of well known local landmarks like the Llandoger Trow. In the late 1960s they were opening a new outlet every month until the total reached 147; some of them were even in Japan.

The menu expanded, and many people now in their sixties remember going out for a Berni with great nostalgia. 'As a young man from a not wealthy family, going out for a steak was a real treat. In fact you'd boast about it at school the next day. My nan and granddad used to treat us to a Berni Inn steak. I was told to always have the fillet steak, as it was the best, and it was like winning the lottery!'

The celebrity chef Nigel Slater also remembers the Berni experience:

> Saturday lunch was a milestone meal in that I was allowed to choose my own dishes from the menu. I stuck safely to things I had seen my parents eat: melon cut into a boat with an orange sail and a maraschino cherry, followed by steak garni, medium rare. 'That'll be very bloody. Are you sure?' my step-mother would ask, followed by a shudder at the thought of it. My dad, for whom a steak should be so raw its veins were still pumping, would say 'Leave him be. He knows what he wants'. Steak garni always sounded so much more exotic than plain steak, despite the fact that the 'garni' was only half a tomato and a bit of cress.

The Llandoger Trow in King Street, one-time flagship of the Berni Inn chain

Eventually the Bernis' success led to predators circling around, and the purchase of their empire in 1970 by the huge conglomerate Grand Metropolitan for £14.5 million. They sold the chain on to Whitbread in 1990 and they changed the name to Beefeater Pubs, presumably because by this time Berni Inns were seen as passé. One restaurant critic described their fare as 'industrial cuisine' and the word 'naff' was frequently used to describe them. They even warranted a reference in the British sci-fi sitcom Red Dwarf: 'Loneliness weighs heavily on us all. Personally, the only thing that keeps me going is the thought that we are over 60 billion miles away from the nearest Berni Inn.' By that time tastes had clearly moved on.

Aldo Berni died in 1997, aged 88. He had been the typical front-of-house man, genial, welcoming and beaming, with a range of extravagant Italian gestures, and he retired very wealthy. Unfortunately, he gave his considerable fortune to his wife Esme, assuming he would die before her. In fact she died first, by a year, and left almost all their £4.8 million to a local home for dogs and cats. His brother Frank was the man behind the scenes, cost-conscious, quiet and hard working. He died in 2000 in Jersey at the age of 96. The Berni brothers, from very small beginnings in the centre of Bristol, created what was then the largest restaurant chain in the world outside America. They were, in their time, great Bristol inventors and innovators.

43 STEAM LOCOMOTIVES

Made by Peckett and Sons

THE FIRM THAT BECAME PECKETT'S was founded by Francis William Fox, who came from Kingsbridge in south Devon. He trained as a railway engineer and in 1864 formed a company in Bristol with Edwin Walker called Fox Walker. They opened an engineering works in Deep Pit Road, St George, next to the Deep Pit coal mine and also, very conveniently, by the side of a branch line which ran from Kingswood Junction to Speedwell Colliery. They gave their factory the rather grandiose name of the Atlas Locomotive Works.

The company concentrated on making small tank engines rather than large, mainline locomotives, and by 1878 it had made a total of 424. It was in financial trouble, however, and in 1881 it was taken over by a Birmingham engineer, Thomas Peckett, who soon brought his four sons into the business. Together they resurrected the company, using many of the Fox, Walker castings until they developed their own. They still concentrated their efforts on tank engines that were 'eminently suitable for branch lines, mineral lines, steel and iron works, gas works, tinplate works, collieries and all kinds of contractors' work'. Their locomotives might not have been glamorous, but during the first half of the twentieth century Pecketts had a sizeable slice of the market. They were not things of beauty – 'dumpy' would best describe them – but with a copper top to their chimney, a big brass dome and a high-roofed driver's cab they looked just like a tank engine should, functional and workmanlike. The Revd Wilbert Awdry was clearly a fan. In his many *Thomas the Tank Engine* books, Percy bears a remarkable resemblance to a Peckett tank engine. Proof of their charm is the fact that there are now railway preservation societies all over the world who are busy restoring, or still running, Peckett locos. The oldest survivor, probably built in 1896, is the property of a railway museum in Kent.

Peckett's exported their locomotives far and wide, to countries as diverse as Sarawak, Sudan, Argentina, Tasmania and Rhodesia. Their heaviest weighed 73 tons and was made specifically for the Christmas Island Phosphate Company, out in the Indian Ocean, south of Indonesia. The story goes that in 1939, as the Japanese army was advancing, the decision was taken to put explosive charges in the cylinders and blow them up, thus making the loco totally inoperative. After the war, the company was asked to supply new cylinders, and before long it was working again, a tribute to the extreme robustness of its products. The company's smallest locomotive was probably the Dwarf. It had two-foot diameter wheels, weighed only 11 tons and was designed for Courtaulds to go under a six-foot bridge at their works in Wales, a feat it achieved with three inches to spare. Over the years, Peckett's are believed to have

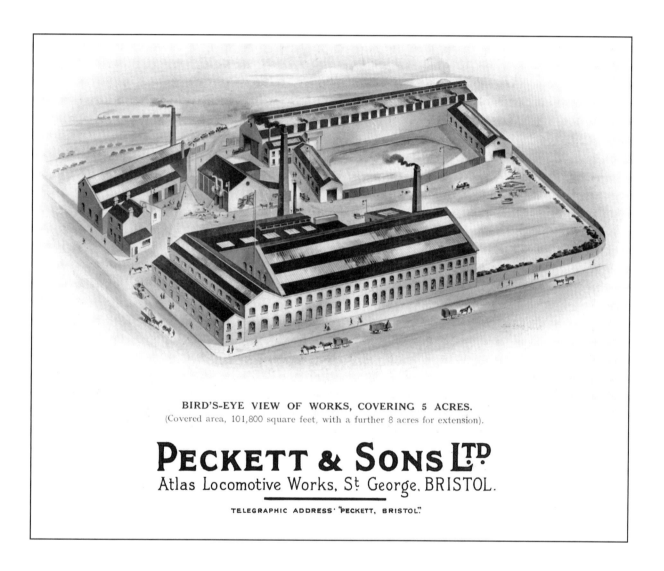

BIRD'S-EYE VIEW OF WORKS, COVERING 5 ACRES.
(Covered area, 101,800 square feet, with a further 8 acres for extension).

PECKETT & SONS L^{TD}
Atlas Locomotive Works, St George, BRISTOL.

TELEGRAPHIC ADDRESS: "PECKETT, BRISTOL."

built between 1,900 and 2,000 locomotives in various shapes and sizes.

After the war, the Atlas works suffered from a lack of raw materials; in 1947, for example, only five new locomotives were made, and part of the factory was given over to stripping salvaged aeroplane engines, of which there were plenty. During the 1950s steam was on its way out but Frank and Wilfred Peckett, George's sons, had Luddite tendencies, and clung to the notion that new diesel locomotives were just a passing fad. When Frank finally retired in 1954, Pecketts announced that they were planning

Peckett & Sons, Ltd.
Atlas Locomotive Works, Bristol.
Telegraphic Address: "Peckett, Bristol."

LOCOMOTIVES

of all sizes and gauges, **specially constructed for Main and Branch Lines,
Shipyards, Contractors, Docks, Gasworks, Collieries** and **Ironworks,**
and for every other variety of service.
Locomotives of various sizes **always in progress** for early delivery.
FULL PARTICULARS ON APPLICATION.

to build their first diesel, but it was too late; other more go-ahead manufacturers had taken over their market. Peckett's only ever built five diesel locos before they finally went bust. Their last steam engine, number 2165, left the Atlas Works on its way to a sugar estate in Mozambique on June 12, 1958 and Peckett and Sons was no more. But

Top: the finishing shop at the
Atlas Works, St George

left: Henbury, built in 1937, on
the quayside near M Shed

if you want to take a trip down memory lane, go down to the harbourside by the Bristol
M Shed in the summer, and see and even travel behind an original Peckett tank engine
called Henbury which was made in 1937.

44 SUBSCRIBER TRUNK DIALLING

Made by Post Office Telephones

FOR ANYONE UNDER THE AGE OF SIXTY the word 'operator' means next to nothing, unless you happen to watch black-and-white films on daytime television. On Friday December 5, 1958, Bristol was partly responsible for making the word, and the person it referred to, obsolete. On that day the Queen made a historic phone call from the Bristol Central Telephone Exchange in the Equity and Law building on Baldwin Street. Bristol was chosen as the city to have Britain's first Subscriber Trunk Dialling exchange partly because it had been home to Britain's first telephone exchange of any kind back in 1879, three years after Alexander Graham Bell had first filed his historic patent; unbelievably, there were only 25 subscribers.

The Queen was invited to mark the occasion by making the country's first automatically dialled trunk call, a 'trunk' call simply meaning 'long distance'. The *Bristol Evening Post* made the most of the occasion and announced, in a special royal edition:

> The Queen in Bristol this afternoon made the country's first twopenny trunk call, thus opening a new telephone service to 18,000 homes on the Bristol Central Exchange.

Apparently Her Majesty amazed 150 specially invited onlookers, and probably herself, by dialling the number 031 CAL 3636, and 365 miles away the Lord Provost of Edinburgh picked up the phone to receive her call. The phone, the *Post* reported, was powder blue in colour and was linked to an electronic robot which the Bristol telephone engineers called Grace. The conversation consisted of the following pleasantries:

> This is the Queen speaking from Bristol. Good afternoon, Lord Provost.

The Lord Provost rather unctuously replied:

> Good afternoon, your Majesty. May I with humble duty offer you the loyal greetings of the City of Edinburgh.

The Queen, perhaps unnecessarily, then explained the reason for her call: 'In a few moments, Bristol subscribers will be able to make trunk calls by merely dialling the right number in a radius of 300 miles. In time, the whole United Kingdom will enjoy the advantage of this new service that the Post Office has introduced.' The call lasted two minutes, five seconds and cost 10d (75p today), although it is doubtful whether

Her Majesty ever paid for it. The Postmaster-General, Ernest Marples, then explained to the Queen that in the near future she would be able to dial Buckingham Palace direct from Windsor Castle without having to enlist the help of an operator. The Queen was suitably impressed, although it was, as she later admitted to the Postmaster General, the first time she had personally dialled a number. It was also the first time a monarch had been photographed holding a telephone!

At the end of her visit, the Queen was presented with the historic powder blue phone, an artefact for future historians to treasure. Fifty years later, on December 5, 2008, a reunion of the telephone engineers working on the new technology was organised by Brian Fox, an 18-year-old at the time. He told the *Evening Post*:

> It was one of the most important days ever in telecommunications history, and a huge amount of work went into making sure the day went without a hitch. We stood between rows of equipment, as close as we could get, and watched Her Majesty dial the number. When it was all over the Duke of Edinburgh remarked: 'You can relax now, chaps, it all works'.

This new service was all part of the Post Office's £35 million campaign to get us to use

HM The Queen making the first STD call, 5 December, 1958, flanked by the Duke of Edinburgh and the Postmaster-General, Ernest Marples our phones more often by making calls easier, faster and cheaper. At the time, in 1958, the average person with a telephone – and millions of families did not own one – made only two calls a day. Compare that with today's mobile user! As a result of this technological advance, more than half of Britain's operators had lost their jobs by 1970, and the last operator service was phased out in 1979. London lagged two years behind Bristol, and did not get STD until 1960.

After that day in Bristol in 1958, dialling a phone number was never the same; and the once space-age acronym STD now means something far less inspiring: sexually transmitted disease.

THREE MEN IN A BOAT 45

Published in Bristol by JW Arrowsmith

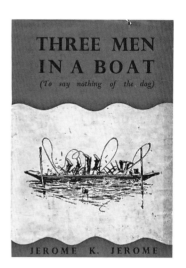

THE PRINTERS AND PUBLISHERS J W Arrowsmith of Quay Street, Bristol specialised in exceedingly dull but moderately profitable railway and steamer timetables. The company, however, wanted to branch out into more general publishing. John Arrowsmith persuaded an estate agent friend called Fred Fargus to write a 'shilling shocker' for him. *Called Back*, written by Fargus under the pen name Hugh Conway, sold thousands. It paved the way for Arrowsmith's to build up a reputation as publishers of popular fiction as well as timetables, and soon well known writers such as Anthony Hope and even Arthur Conan Doyle had signed contracts with them.

Jerome K Jerome, the son of an ironmonger, was born in Walsall but brought up in east London. He left school at 14 and worked as a clerk, actor, schoolmaster and journalist until he wrote a moderately successful humorous book called *Idle Thoughts of an Idle Fellow*. His next planned project was provisionally called *The Story of the Thames*, and it was to be a far more serious book; but the comic interludes he inserted soon took over and the book was retitled because, as Jerome later wrote, 'Half way through I hit upon *Three Men in a Boat*, because nothing else seemed right'. The book was based on numerous trips on the Thames Jerome had made with two friends, George Wingrave and Carl Hentschel – renamed William Samuel Harris by Jerome. In the story he 'recorded events that really happened. All that has been done is to colour them, and for this no extra charge is made'. The dog, though, was a figment of Jerome's imagination: 'Montmorency evolved out of my inner consciousness.' In 1888 the story was first published as a magazine serial, but when it came to releasing it in book form, Jerome decided to switch publishers because he judged Arrowsmith's 'for energy and push, I suppose clearly the leading publisher'. In fact he was equally commercially minded, and persuaded Arrowsmith's to publish his book for 3s 6d (decimal equivalent 17p) instead of 1s (5p).

When it first came out, reviewers slated it. *The Standard*, Jerome wrote later:

> spoke of me as a menace to English letters. I think I may claim to have been, for the first 20 years of my career, the best abused author in England.

The posh papers clearly thought it vulgar. *The Morning Post* described the book as 'an example of the sad results to be expected from the over-education of the lower orders.' *The Times* very sniffily said it was written in 'colloquial clerk's English... designed to appeal to 'Arrys and 'Arriets'. Even the humorous magazine *Punch* was, according to Jerome, 'especially indignant'. 'One might have imagined, to read some of the critics,

J. W. ARROWSMITH, *Printer and Publisher,*
11 Quay Street, Bristol.

SKETCH OF STONE BRIDGE, SHOWING ST. JOHN'S CHURCH.
(From Drawing by J. A. Sandeson, circa 1820.)
(Showing the premises now occupied by J. W. Arrowsmith, the Printer and Publisher of The "Official Guide to the City of Bristol.")

QUAY STREET, SHOWING ST. JOHN'S CHURCH. PRESENT DAY.
(Catalogue of Publications will be sent post free on request.)

that the British Empire was in danger'. Jerome himself admitted it was not a literary masterpiece: 'What readers ask nowadays in a book is that it should improve, instruct and elevate. This book wouldn't elevate a cow.' He simply hit on a winning formula – pick a journey, any journey, as a skeleton, and then tell as many funny stories as you can make to fit. It worked wonderfully well, although the structure of the book was admittedly unsatisfactory. The three men do not get into their boat until a third of the way through the book, and the return journey takes only a very rushed 11 pages. Happily, readers all over the world recognised that it is a story of three very ordinary but accident-prone young men having a good time together, a kind of Victorian *Men Behaving Badly*, a series of adventures which also happened to cash in on the contemporary craze for boating. It has been translated into languages as different as Hebrew, Japanese and Portuguese. For some strange reason, it was especially popular in Germany and Russia.

Three Men in a Boat might have sold millions of copies, but Jerome did not quite become a millionaire, because many of the overseas sales were of pirated copies for which he did not receive a penny. To date the book has sold more than three million copies in its English language edition alone, and it is still going strong. It has been made into a film three times, a stage musical and in 2006 a television series starring Griff Rhys Jones, Dara O'Briain and Rory McGrath. Had Mr Arrowsmith not accepted it for publication, it would have been the literary equivalent of Decca turning down the Beatles. Years later, commenting on the amount of royalties he paid Jerome, he confessed he was at a loss to know what became of all the copies of *Three Men in a Boat*. 'I often think,' he said, 'that the public must eat them'.

Published by Alastair Sawday

ALASTAIR SAWDAY IS A ONE-OFF – a green activist, formidable networker and tireless campaigner for all things ecological who has also ended up a very successful publisher of travel books; so much so that if you are the sort of person who reads the *Guardian* or *Independent* you will almost certainly have read at least one of his books on saving the planet and stayed at many of his recommended bed and breakfasts or hotels, both in this country and abroad.

Alastair moved to Bristol in 1975 and has been living in the same house in 'Lower' Clifton ever since. In 1984, after teaching and then working for Friends of the Earth and the Green Party, he started a small travel company taking very trusting American tourists in a minibus on guided tours all over France, Spain, Portugal and Italy. He prided himself on taking his clients to stay in really out-of-the-way places, and on giving them an authentic taste of those countries rather than fobbing them off with the obvious package-tour itineraries that most rival companies offered. This gave him the idea of publishing a guide to off-the-beaten-track places to stay in France. For this he used his family and friends as researchers and in 1994 his first book, *Special Places to Stay: French Bed and Breakfast* was published. From those small beginnings he has never really looked back. A guide to special bed and breakfasts and then small hotels in Britain followed, and then similar guides to countries like Ireland, Italy, Spain, Portugal, Greece and Turkey. He now publishes guides to far-away places such as Morocco and even India and the Sawday brand is now so strong it even appears on, and presumably helps to sell, tubs of Anchor butter and cartons of Tropicana fruit juice.

To begin with, Alastair worked from offices in a small terrace house in Clifton-wood. In 2006 he moved into new über-eco-friendly offices in a collection of converted barns in Yanley, just outside Long Ashton, where he now employs 40 people, most of them women. His son Toby, who looks like a younger clone of his father, now works for the business, and as managing director has taken over a lot of the day-to-day decision-making. Still chairman, Alastair Sawday prides himself on being greener than green. Until recently he ran his very small car on recycled cooking oil from fish and chip shops, despite the fact that stray bits of fish or the occasional chip clogged the filters. Not to worry, he usually cycles to work anyway.

Some critics suggest that his books encourage people to take to planes or cars and so contribute to global warming. His travel guides also have a very ungreen habit of rapidly becoming obsolescent, since new, revised editions of the British books come out every year, and for most of the others it is every other year. You can, however, access all the information they contain for free via the Sawday website, which is some-

Alastair Sawday outside his eco-friendly offices just outside Long Ashton

thing of a problem when your business is trying to sell books. The very short shelf life is necessary because about 10 per cent of the entries drop out every year; owners retire or move on to something else, while about five per cent are struck off each year as a result of Sawday's receiving negative reports. These are then followed up with anonymous visits, and if the complaints seem justified, the owners are told the bad news. One couple were so distraught at the implications it had for their business, they threatened to sue Sawday Publishing. The case never came to court.

Nowadays, so many people use the guides that several owners of small hotels and B&Bs are completely dependent on them for their business, and the entry fee they have to pay, usually between £300 and £600 a year, is money very well spent. So how do they qualify for inclusion, and what exactly is 'special' about Alastair Sawday's *Special Places to Stay*? The man himself is the best person to answer that. He says:

> Chain hotels, conference facilities and customer relations executives leave me cold. A lot of the writing in 'accommodation' guides makes me wince. The magical thing about our books is that their sales have revealed to me that there are hundreds of thousands of people who feel exactly the same. So we try to be the guide for those looking for warm, very human, interesting people, beautiful buildings, original style, elegant simplicity and fine old things that, however dilapidated, carry their age and authenticity with dignity. Then there is delicious

food, much of it grown at home and cooked with devotion, comfort, but not at the expense of everything else, and a touch of fun with a touch of class – quirkiness with seriousness, a light touch, an easy style.

In other words, Sawday books are very, very different from AA guides. In fact if a place gets the thumbs up from the AA, it will probably get the thumbs down from Alastair Sawday. His books spend a lot of time and purple prose describing the owners, the warmth of their welcome, their dogs, cats, chickens or even donkeys, the quality of the wine they offer you, their choice of paintings or colour schemes and above all the atmosphere of the place. As the *Guardian* put it:

> Alastair Sawday guides are designed to give you the feel of a place, as though you were visiting it as friends, not as potential customers.

In brief, whether they are in Europe or further afield, jaw-droppingly expensive or heart-warmingly cheap, they all pass the unique Sawday test of being very special.

Made by Fry's

LIKE A LOT OF ADVERTISING SLOGANS, 'Full of Eastern Promise' could not be much further from the truth. Fry's Turkish Delight might have an exotic name but until very recently it was made in Bristol, or Keynsham, which for the purposes of this book is near enough. It is a very traditional brand, a bit like Marmite – you either like it or loathe it. It is sweet, almost sickly sweet, some people would say, and it has a rather jelly-like consistency. One American commentator decided that 'it tasted like jelly from a jelly fish', although that was presumably a matter of guesswork on his part. Then again, if you are a fan of Turkish Delight, you have probably been a fan for life. The brand first appeared as long ago as 1914, perhaps not an auspicious year to launch a new product, but it was an instant success. For many Bristolians it is good to see that the name Fry's lives on, even though the only other product that still carries the name is Fry's Chocolate Cream.

The history of chocolate can be traced back to when Christopher Columbus returned to Spain from the Americas for the fourth time in 1502, bringing with him cocoa beans he had obtained from some obliging Aztecs. For the next century the Spanish nobility managed to keep the secret of how to make sweet cocoa from bitter cocoa beans, but after that the taste for it gradually spread and came to the notice of Dr Joseph Fry. Born in Sutton Benger, near Chippenham, and apprenticed to an apothecary in Basingstoke, he came to Bristol and opened an apothecary's shop in Small Street in 1748. Chocolate in those days was thought to have medicinal qualities – for some people it still does – and Fry found himself dispensing more and more of it for his patients. His trade card extolled the virtues of:

> Fry's Genuine Patent Cocoa which has continued in the highest repute for many yeares and is recommended in preference to every other kind of Breakfast to such who have tender habits, decayed health, weak lungs or nervous or scorbutic tendencies.

By 1756 Fry was manufacturing his own chocolate on a small scale, which increased in 1761 when he bought the patent rights to a chocolate-making engine invented by a Bristolian, Walter Churchman. In 1777 Fry's moved into a new factory in Union Street, and remained in that area for the next 150 years. Despite the alleged medicinal qualities of the product that made his fortune, Joseph died in 1787 at the relatively early age of 59, leaving his wife to take over the business and rename it Anna Fry and

The Fry's factory in Union Street and the Pithay in the centre of Bristol

Sons. By 1822 Fry's were using nearly 40 per cent of all the chocolate imported into Britain, and expansion continued. By 1866 Fry's employed 350 workers, and by 1904 this had mushroomed to 4,600. For more than half a century, the delicious smell of warm, melting chocolate mingled with the aroma of hops from George's brewery on the other side of Bristol Bridge.

According to a report written by Mr J Edward White in 1865, conditions in the Fry's Union Street factory were exemplary:

> The rooms are airy and cheerful. Cleanliness prevails. The younger girls whom I spoke to had all been at school and said they could read. Some girls sent down to me all read nicely from a magazine, except one who made mistakes, as it seemed from nervousness.

True to Joseph Fry's Quaker beliefs, the rules for Fry's employees were strict, in fact positively repressive by today's standards: 'All male staff are instructed that all unnecessary familiarity with the opposite sex is to be avoided at all costs. Employees are warned that they are on no account to wander idly from department to department and those found singing, eating the firm's goods, entering beer shops outside working hours or acting with any impropriety are subject to the firm's and the family's strict censure.'

Fry's merged with Cadbury's in 1917, and over the years its name

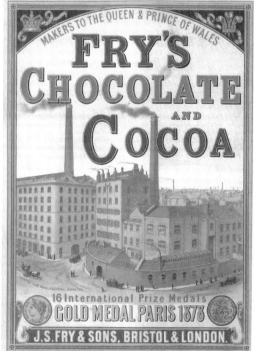

A SOUVENIR OF
SOMERDALE

FRY'S MAKERS OF GOOD CHOCOLATE

J. S. FRY & SONS LTD., SOMERDALE, BRISTOL.

has gradually been dropped. Cadbury's Turkish Delight, however, just would not sound right.

The massive red-brick Somerdale factory at Keynsham was started in 1923 on a 228-acre green-field site on water meadows by the river Avon. The move out of central Bristol took until 1935 to complete, although the demolition of the Fry's factories was started in 1932. Two tall chimneys remained standing in the Pithay until the 1960s, despite the blitz. The name Somerdale was chosen as the result of a national competition, and when finished the factory had its own railway sidings, sports fields and Fry Hall, where conferences were held and plays and pantos put on.

Since then, millions of chocolate bars in all shapes and sizes have poured from its production lines. Until recently, approximately 1,000 people worked at the Keynsham factory, producing 50,000 tonnes of chocolate products a year. Turkish Delight was probably the best known, and millions of bars of it emerged from the factory every week, in the traditional purple wrapping with 'Turkish Delight' written in a style vaguely Middle Eastern. In the 1960s it became especially popular as a result of an advertising campaign featuring a well known model and actress called Jane Lumb. The *Liverpool Post* described her as having, 'long legs, a short skirt, a come-hither pout and a boarding school voice'. Whatever her attributes, she did wonders for sales, and they again soared in 2006 to more than a million a week when a film of C S Lewis's *Chronicles of Narnia* came out, featuring children who would gladly sell their siblings to an evil witch just to get their hands on more Turkish Delight. The boy hero Edmund was described by Lewis as 'trying to shovel down as much Turkish Delight as he could, and the more he ate, the more he wanted'.

So what is so special about Fry's Turkish Delight? Apparently it contains a magic ingredient – otto – an oil made from rose petals, according to Cadbury's advertising people, who also describe it as 'a mystical, exotic treat that lets you escape from the everyday'. The story goes that it started with a Turkish confectioner by the name of Hadji Bekir in the eighteenth century. He devised a new, soft and chewy concoction from water, sugar, cornflour and lemon cream of tartar. Left to simmer for an hour, it was then sprinkled with rose water before being allowed to cool. Dusted with powdered sugar, it was finally cut up into bite-sized chunks. No mention of chocolate: that was Fry's addition. Hadji Bekir called his creation 'rahat lokhoum', or 'soothing to the throat', but that does not exactly trip off the English tongue, so Turkish Delight was called upon as an extremely loose translation. Back in Istanbul, the sultan and his harem were so keen on the new concoction that Hadji Bekir was appointed chief confectioner to the palace. A shop in Istanbul is still owned and run by his descendants, who take a dim view of the suggestion that Turkish Delight was invented by a Greek. Wherever it originated, both Napoleon and Winston Churchill were fans, and the product kept thousands of people in the Bristol area in work.

Nowadays, Cadbury Schweppes claim that Turkish Delight has 'the lowest fat content of any of our bars', so it could theoretically be part of a calorie-controlled diet, as well as benefiting your health in the way chocolate did Dr Fry's first customers. A wonder bar, then, but unfortunately one with no longer any connection with the Bristol area. The link was finally cut in 2011, when the Somerdale factory was closed with the loss of 400 jobs after the company was taken over by the American conglomerate Kraft Foods.

48

WALLACE AND GROMIT FILMS

Made by Aardman Animations

Peter Lord

TWO BOYS, PETER LORD AND DAVID SPROXTON, met at school when they were 13 and discovered that they shared a hobby – animation. It remained a hobby until after they left school when they made a very, very short (20-second) cartoon which featured a deadpan super-hero who for some reason they named Aardman. A few months later they managed to sell one of his adventures to a BBC television programme called *Vision On*. And the rest is history, except that Aardman Animations is very far from being history.

In 1976 the two friends set up their company in Bristol, and the following year they created a character made of modelling clay which they called Morph to appear in another BBC programme, *Take Hart*. He immediately caught on and very soon went on to star in his own series *The Amazing Adventures of Morph*, which has become cult viewing for people of all ages.

From the start, Lord and Sproxton were determined not to be just creators of programmes for children's television. They wanted to prove that animated films could appeal equally to adults, and a series for Channel 4 called *Conversation Pieces* proved they were right. Nick Park joined the Aardman team in 1985, after he had invited Lord and Sproxton to give a short seminar on animation at the National Film School, where he was a student. Afterwards they spoke and learned that Nick had for years been working on a short film which he had been inspired to make after seeing Morph. Because he was doing everything himself he had only managed to make six minutes of it. Eventually the three agreed to finish it together. The result was *A Grand Day Out*, which alongside Nick's five-minute film *Creature Comforts* won an Oscar nomination and an Academy Award.

Wallace and Gromit soon became household names with *The Wrong Trousers* (1993) and *A Close Shave* (1995). The feature film *Chicken Run* followed in 2000 and grossed over $220 million worldwide – anything but chicken feed. This was followed in 2005 by Aardman's greatest hit to date, *The Curse of the Were-Rabbit*, which took five years to make and also won Aardman an Academy Award. Its stars are again Wallace, an eccentric, cheese-loving inventor from Lancashire and his long-suffering mongrel dog Gromit. The plot sounds a million miles from your average Hollywood blockbuster:

> Wallace and his loyal dog Gromit set out to discover the mystery behind the garden sabotage that plagues their village and threatens the annual giant vegetable growing contest.

Nick Park says Wallace is based loosely on his dad, an incurable tinkerer, and has also said:

> I think people see Wallace and Gromit as something akin to an elderly couple. These two know each other so well. Nothing can split them… Maybe I love Gromit because he's the dog I've never had. What dog could match him? He's the ideal. He doesn't bark and he has tea and dinner ready for you when you arrive home.

The *Were-Rabbit* film is packed with very British visual and verbal jokes: Gromit, for example, is seen reading a paper with the headline, 'Dog Reads Paper', and owns a collection of records by Bach.

That aside, it is the models of Wallace and Gromit that are the real stars. At their studios in Gas Ferry Road, just behind the ss *Great Britain*, Aardman have to make as many as 35 basic Wallaces, 45 Gromits and four or five different models for most other characters for a typical film. They are made mostly of modelling clay but inside each is a metal 'armature', a bit like a strong but flexible skeleton which can be easily manipulated by the animators. Each model must be firmly fixed to the floor so that it does not fall over, and can be made to adopt quite extreme positions. The model of Lady Tottington, for instance, has a very unladylike length of metal descending to the floor between her legs, although this is obviously invisible to the audience. Wallace has a hard plastic resin tank top which gives the animators something solid to hold on to while his head can be pulled off to change his mouth shape and expression. Wallace's face, in particular, comes in for a huge amount of reworking, because the mouth shape has to be changed for every syllable he speaks. To make it simpler, the animators have a different mouth for every sound he is ever likely to utter. Even with 30 cameras and 30 animators working on 30 different sets, it can take a week to produce a minute or two of film.

It has not all been plain sailing for Aardman. Nick Park managed to lose vital models of Wallace and Gromit when he left them in a New York taxi cab in 1995. Fortunately, the driver looked in the boot two days later, found them, returned them and even refused the $500 reward Park had offered. Then, on October 10, 2005, a fire swept through the storage warehouse at the old John Lysaght headquarters in Silverthorne Lane and destroyed some of 30 years' output of props, models and scenery. Nick Park commented: 'Even though it's a precious and nostalgic collection and valuable to the company, in the light of other tragedies, today isn't a big deal.'

A deal with a major Hollywood studio DreamWorks, founded by Steven Spielberg, produced *Chicken Run* and helped make *The Curse of the Were-Rabbit* a huge hit on both sides of the Atlantic. The film won Bafta awards as well as an Ocar, but after working together for ten years, it was announced in 2006 that 'due to creative differences DreamWorks Animation and Aardman would not be extending their contract. The business model of DreamWorks no longer suits Aardman and vice versa, but the split could not have been more amicable'. Whatever the reason, Aardman now have a feature contract with Sony.

Aardman's most recent Wallace and Gromit film, *A Matter of Loaf and Death*, was shown by the BBC on Christmas Day in 2008. More than 16 million people watched it and deemed it a huge hit. Now it is just a question of waiting for the duo's next cracking adventure…

WIGS

49

Made by Peter Owen and Company

THERE ARE NOT MANY FIRMS in Bristol that are so internationally famous that they can afford not to have their name in the Bristol phone book or even the local Yellow Pages. But one such firm is Peter Owen and Company. To find it you have to walk down a back alley sandwiched between Cotham Hill and Whiteladies Road, and even then you could easily miss it, since the sign on the door is very discreet. Then, when you walk through the anonymous-looking front door, you are immediately confronted by stacks of shoe boxes, each with a different name scribbled on it, and it is these names that make you step back. They are all Hollywood superstars or A-list celebs, and inside each of the boxes is a very precise plastic mould of that person's head, ready to be used at any time to make a perfectly fitting wig or hairpiece.

The anonymous-looking building in a back street in Cotham where Peter Owen wigs are created

Peter Owen, the company's founder, was born in Bristol but left as a small baby, returning years later to study at Bristol University. While there he got involved in student drama productions and also worked part-time at the Old Vic, going there full-time after graduating. After that he worked on costume dramas for London Weekend Television and the BBC, and then for the Welsh National Opera. He says he was learning how to 'change what people look like'. That included wigs, make-up, false noses, wrinkles, scratches, gashes, bags and boils; and as there was no text book, he learned it all from experience, through trial and error.

His big Hollywood breakthrough came when Vanessa Redgrave, with whom he had worked, put into the contract for her next film that she must have him doing her make-up and wigs. This was a tall order since she was to play the part of a trans-sexual, changing unusually from a woman to a bearded man. The result was so successful that Owen soon acquired a reputation in Hollywood. Michelle Pfeifer, Keira Knightley, Nicole Kidman, Johnny Depp, Nicholas Cage, Kate Winslet, Bruce Willis and Meryl Streep all now insist that Peter Owen is ready, willing and able to work with them on their next movie, while Oprah Winfrey reportedly wears a Peter Owen wig for every show she makes.

In Bristol the company had an office and workshop in Denmark Street until it moved to Cotham in 1998. Bristol was chosen because Peter never really felt at home in London or Los Angeles: 'It's great to live somewhere that's not as oppressive as London. It's easier to get around, easier to work and with modern technology it doesn't really matter where you are. That's why I live in the city I love. It's very civilised and beautiful.' Nevertheless, it is still a bit odd to think that people like Cameron Diaz might sometimes have to find their way to a Bristol back alley to have a wig fitting.

Upstairs in the office, film scripts of the next Hollywood blockbuster are left lying around on the table next to the coffee machine, and the walls are covered in photographs of various actors, together with handwritten notes of appreciation. As confirmation of the company's success there is also a scattering of Oscars and Bafta awards. If any further confirmation was needed, the phone rang during our interview: a call from Robert de Niro's agent. Could Peter Owen work for him on his next movie? A moment's thought and then came the response: 'Sorry. Too busy.' They can afford to turn down potential clients like that. By his own admission, Peter Owen is very, very expensive, although he does what he describes as a Rolls Royce job. In the multi-million-dollar budget for a big movie, however, the cost of his company's work is relatively small. In contrast, its visual impact is crucial.

The work is hard and sometimes stressful. Getting temperamental actors on to the set all made up and on time is not easy. Some shoots can be happy, others less so, but the atmosphere in the office and the workshop is very relaxed. According to Peter Owen, 'We're more like a big family than a business'. Ten people work for the company, Peter, his co-director Jessica and the highly-skilled people whose job it is to create the wigs.

The hair for them comes mainly from Russia and other eastern European countries, where peasant women still traditionally wear long plaits. Many are so poor that for a few roubles they are more than willing to chop off their hair; after all, it will soon grow back again. Peter Owen is obliged to buy it from Russian 'businessmen' who act as wholesalers. Good quality human hair costs £1,500 a kilo, and it has to be bought 40 kilos at a time. The hard, creative work starts in the workshop, with each plait or

The heads of just a very few of the film actors for whom Peter Owen has made wigs

bundle of hair sorted and then blended. A good quality wig is often made from the hair of as many as six or seven different women, and each strand has to be meticulously knotted into place.

When it comes to fitting the wigs on film sets, the worst kind of actors to work with are apparently those who use the word 'I' or 'me' in such phrases as 'I don't think

Ian McKellen, *Lord of the Rings*

it suits me'. More preferable are the ones who are only concerned that the wig or make-up suits the character they are playing. The most interesting jobs are generally the most challenging. *Lord of the Rings*, for example, presented the formidable task of creating the look of an entire set of other-worldly characters, ranging from Gandalf and Saruman to various elves and hobbits. It was hard work, as Peter Owen later commented:

> It was like organising World War III. They were shooting in never less than three places simultaneously. We had six weeks to prepare everything, which was ridiculous. We had to design the make-up and create more than a hundred new wigs. There was no time to panic. But it worked. Do people realise that everyone in the film is wearing a wig? All the beards are false, plus there are false noses and ears everywhere. It's an odd craft, wig-making, because to be recognised in the industry, you have to make wigs look so real that nobody realises they're wigs. I consider myself to be a bit of a forger, and it's nice to get away with it.

Once filming begins, Peter hovers behind the cameras, making sure the wigs look natural. Each one has a double in case of accidents: 'You'd be foolish to start filming with only one wig. They take over three weeks to make, and you can't hold up filming for that long.' Apparently the ideal film to work on is one where the director agrees to 'give us the chance to help tell the story'. Peter Owen and his team are obviously very good at doing just that.

It is a long way from Hollywood to Hampton Lane, Cotham but it is clear that this is a company that manages to work comfortably and very successfully in both places.

WILDLIFE PROGRAMMES

50

Made by the BBC Natural History Unit

THE AMERICAN MAGAZINE *Time* recently noted how important Bristol is, in one respect at least: 'No pride of lions prowls its streets, no shiver of sharks cruises its river, but the small English city of Bristol (pop. 380,000) has built a global reputation as a center of wildlife filmmaking.'

Johnny Morris in *Animal Magic*

But why Bristol, you might ask, and the answer is pure luck, and one that perfectly illustrates the old saying 'Mighty oaks from little acorns grow'. During the Second World War the BBC's drama, religious and variety departments were hurriedly evacuated from London and many programmes were broadcast from the depths of the Clifton Rocks Railway, half way up the side of the Clifton Gorge. One young BBC radio producer, Desmond Hawkins, happened to be interested in natural history so when, just after the war, the head of the BBC in Bristol, an ex-teacher from Taunton called Frank Gillard, was casting around for ideas for programmes to justify the corporation's continued existence in Bristol, Hawkins suggested a series of radio programmes which later came to be known as *The Naturalist*.

The first programme was broadcast on June 4, 1946 on the Home Service. Despite its decidedly uncatchy title it proved popular and by the time Desmond Hawkins climbed the greasy pole at the BBC and became Head of Programmes, West Region, the unit was well and truly established. Nevertheless, he realised that natural history programmes made for radio, with names like *Birdsong of the Month*, were of limited appeal because they lacked pictures – so although relatively few people had television sets, the BBC had the foresight to set up its Natural History Unit in Bristol in 1957. In truth, at this time, the unit had very few pictures to show. Producers were more or less dependent on rich friends with their own film cameras who were asked to send in footage shot while on holiday. The clips were often very short and the technical quality was sometimes appalling, which meant that the early programmes had to be padded out with a lot of talking heads back in the Whiteladies Road studio. At the time, even footage from BBC cameramen was usually shot on a wind-up Bolex camera which could run for a maximum of only 28 seconds. Nevertheless, the idea caught on, and prestigious names like Sir Peter Scott, founder of the Wildfowl Trust at Slimbridge and the World Wildlife Fund, helped to lend authority to the new department. Later, *Animal Magic*, with its much-loved presenter Johnny Morris, helped to popularise the work of the Natural History Unit.

The advent of colour television in the late 1960s was a massive boost, and over the years that followed the BBC Natural History Unit had many huge successes. Its first real blockbuster, *Life on Earth*, was shown in 1979. It was filmed in 39 countries and featured 650 different species. Viewing figures were astonishing: more than 15 million people regularly tuned in, and ultimately 500 million-plus people watched it worldwide. Memorable moments included Sir David Attenborough 'playing' with a group of young mountain gorillas, one of which checked his head for fleas. Speaking in a whisper for fear of rousing the nearby parents, he commented:

> There is more meaning and mutual understanding in exchanging a glance with a gorilla than any other animal I know. It seems very unfair that man should have chosen the gorilla to symbolise everything that is aggressive and violent, when that is one thing the gorilla is not – and we are.

At that moment a huge male gorilla raced past him and thumped a female in the back. Commenting later on the fact that he was grimacing at the time, he said: 'I was doing that because out of shot these baby gorillas started taking my shoes off.'

More blockbusters followed, most of them presented by Sir David. With typical modesty he summed up his role thus: 'I am just the tip of the iceberg. I am the public face of what is a very big body of work.' One of the biggest successes to date has been *Planet Earth*, first shown in 2006. The series was different in many ways. In particular it was the animals that were the stars, not the presenters. David Attenborough did not appear on camera, we only heard his voice.

It is clear that we never tire of wildlife programmes. One might think by now that people had had enough of, for example, watching a lion at full speed and an antelope ducking and diving in a desperate attempt to escape, but with *Planet Earth* they managed to come up with a number of variations. For example, one camera crew trekked for weeks in the foothills of the Himalayas in search of the extremely rare and elusive mountain leopard. Just as they were about to give up, they spotted one and filmed it leaping from rock to rock and then half-falling down the side of a mountain in pursuit of a mountain goat. Its teeth sunk into the back leg of its hapless prey – but then, against all the odds, the goat wrenched itself free and dived into a raging river to float away to freedom. The footage was typical of *Planet Earth* – unique.

The series took four years to make and was billed as 'the largest, most expensive' natural history programme ever made. Teams of highly experienced professional cameramen flew off to all corners of the globe, and technically it was significant as the first wildlife series to use HD (high definition) photography. This involved taking very complex, expensive cameras to places where cameras should never go, from freezing mountain tops to steaming rainforests to piranha-infested river beds. In one memorable sequence the cameraman was filming a pack of wolves chasing after a herd of more than three million caribou in the wild and empty north of Canada, from the vantage point of a helicopter flying more than 400 metres above them. The camera then zoomed in to get amazing high-definition close-ups of the chasing wolves.

That sequence was a huge success, but the film crews also experienced failure. One cameraman spent a year tracking penguins in the frozen wastes of the Antarctic. After battling through a blizzard he finally managed to get close enough to film thousands of them huddling together for warmth when temperatures were down to minus 40°C. It was the shot he had been waiting for – but then his camera jammed and the chance was lost. 'I could have cried if my eyes hadn't been frozen,' he said.

An interesting feature of many BBC Natural History programmes is the fact that after 50 minutes they change gear, and the cameramen who took the pictures describe the trials and tribulations they experienced while shooting. These ten minutes can be among the most compelling, but they are there for a very down-to-earth reason. A lot of the money for the programmes is put up by North American co-producers such as the Discovery Channel, who want to allow for ten minutes of commercial breaks. The BBC has to find something else to fill in those ten minutes, and the behind-the-scenes stories are the answer.

In 2007, as a result of government cuts to the annual licence fee, the BBC decided that it was necessary to slash £12 million from the NHU's £37 million annual budget. Fifty seven out of 180 members of staff lost their jobs. Nonetheless, shows like *Natural World* and *Nature's Great Events* keep coming, and the NHU remains one of the jewels in the BBC crown. Today it makes more than 80 hours of television a year, seen in 100-plus countries around the world; and most impressive of all, at least a quarter of all the natural history programmes shown globally originate here in Bristol. As *Time* magazine rather apocalyptically commented: 'If a nuclear bomb went off in Bristol, natural history film programs the world over would be crippled.' What a thought on which to end this book.

Sir David Attenborough, veteran broadcaster and presenter of many of the Natural History Unit's most famous programmes

Acknowledgements

I would like to thank the following for reading through the draft proofs of this book and offering advice, ideas, further suggestions and corrections:

Simon Bartlett of the Bristol Beer Factory. Richard Burley at the Bristol Record Office. Harry Baumer, old friend and ex-Bristolian. Marcus Brearley of Thomas Ware and Sons. Gerry Brooke of the *Bristol Evening Post* whose weekly *Bristol Times* was often an invaluable source of information and ideas. Roger Buoy of Guilberts Chocolates. Dr Francis Burroughs at Bristol Blue Glass (South West). Peter Coate, son of Redvers Coate of Coates Cider, the source of much fascinating information about his father and many fine photographs. Hannah and Don Cameron of Cameron Balloons. Stefan Cembrowicz, a Bristol Car owner and enthusiast. John and Roger Clark and Keith Prested of Clark's Pies. Margot Cooper of Limbs & Things. Martin Curtis, expert on all things to do with Bristol buses. Peter Dunscombe, a friend and expert on the Dunscombe family history. Tim Ewin at Bristol City Museum who told me about the origins of celestine. George Ferguson of the Bristol Beer Factory who tolerated frequent references to his (in)famous red trousers. Tristan Gemmill, actor in *Casualty* and supplier of inside knowledge. David Hardill at the Yate Heritage Centre. Lucy Hepworth, grand-daughter of Redvers Coate. Tristan Hogg, Jon and Romany Simon of Pieminister. Simon Howard of Bailey Caravans. Bob Jones, City archaeologist and expert on mustard gas at Avonmouth. Andy King at the Bristol Museums Service who very kindly checked through the typescript for factual errors. It's down to him that a number of errors were caught in time. Those still remaining are down to me. Ian Learner a good friend who, under duress, did his homework. Catherine Littlejohns at Blaise Castle House Museum. John Oldland and his colleagues at the Kingswood Heritage Museum, a source of many photographs and much useful information. Peter Owen of Peter Owen & Co. Angela Payne at Bristol Blue Glass South West. John Penny, local historian and generous supplier of many of the illustrations in this book. John Raymond-Barker and Ben Pitcher at RB Boatbuilders. Mark Rolt at the Bristol Classic Boat Company. Gabrielle Ruffle at Aardman. Alastair and Toby Sawday of Alastair Sawday Publications. Toby Silverton, owner of Bristol Cars. Sue Storey of BBC Natural History Unit. Rob Swindells, suggestor of many of the entries in this book. Mark Tucker who encouraged me to contact Redcliffe Press. Joe Verrecchia, the source of much information about the Verrecchia family. Alan White of Guilberts Chocolates. Michael Whitton who took the trouble to read and criticise the first draft of the book. David and Tom Whyte who were honest enough to tell me which products were not worth including.

I'd also like to thank my children Anna, Lisa, Luke and Katherine, and particularly my wife Hilary, who have (almost) never tired of hearing me re-tell for the umpteenth time the stories I've unearthed. My thanks also go to John Sansom of Redcliffe Press who responded immediately and very positively to my original suggestion for the book. He then waited very patiently while I researched and wrote it. Many thanks also to Stephen Morris for doing such a fine job on the design. Finally I'd like to thank my good friend Steve Stunt who has given up a huge amount of his time (for free!) to take many of the photographs in this book.

A few howlers, or at least factual errors, have probably still slipped through the net and for these I apologise. I would be grateful for any further information on any of the products and am quite prepared to stand corrected if I've got something wrong. Please contact me at Redcliffe Press: info@redcliffepress.co.uk, 0117 973 7207.

David Bolton, October 2011

M shed

Bristol's new city history museum

In 2011 Bristol's new city history museum opened its doors on Prince's Wharf in the former city docks. M Shed tells the story of the growth of the city from humble beginnings (c.1,000 years ago) to being one of the most important trading and manufacturing cities in the kingdom outside London.

Ham Green pottery, about 1125-1350

This jug is an example from one of the earliest potteries that we know about in the Bristol area. It was found at Ham Green, near Pill. We know that its wares were exported to Ireland because fragments have been found there that match pieces discovered at the Ham Green site

This history is told through the eyes of the residents and visitors to the city and illustrated by objects and archives from the rich and varied collections held in the City Council's museums and Bristol Record Office, collectively known as Bristol Museums, Galleries & Archives.

The town at the bridge (Brigstowe) has seen it all: success and failure, poverty and riches, growth and constriction, innovation and stagnation, immigration and emigration. It has had its fair share of controversy, especially its role in the abhorrent trans-Atlantic slave trade in the eighteenth century but has also contributed enormously to the good of society, from the somewhat esoteric such as Paul Dirac's equation predicting the existence of anti-matter, to the more mundane such as the invention of self-raising flour by the baker Henry Jones.

The spectrum of activity and experiences of life witnessed in the city across time are immense. M Shed picks out important stories reflecting this history and tells them through the eyes of the people who were there.

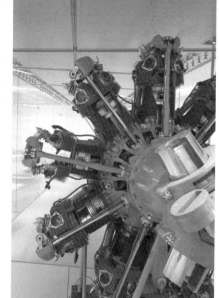

Pegasus engine model

Aero engine designed in 1932 by Roy Fedden and L F 'Bunny' Butler. Over 30,000 Pegasus engines were made up to the mid-1940s

Humphry Davy and laughing gas. An advertisement for laughing gas demonstrations in the 1840s

The Wills family and tobacco

Bristol was the largest centre for tobacco products in Britain for a century before 1980. The Wills family pioneered the manufacture and branding of machine-made cigarettes. They introduced machine-made cigars, Wills Whiffs, in the 1930s, as well as a hand-made range. Tobacco production in Bristol came to an end in 2009

William Friese-Greene
1885-1921

Bristol-born William Friese-Greene was a prolific inventor who registered over 70 patents during his lifetime. He is sometimes credited with being the first person to make a moving film, but most experts dispute this. Even so, he should be remembered as one of the pioneers experimenting with the idea

Perhaps best known for tobacco, boats, planes, cars, glass and ceramics, Bristol has actually seen the manufacture of a huge variety of different goods over time. The objects displayed in M Shed reflect that and include iconic pieces such as the ground breaking 'Lodekker' Bristol double-decker bus, objects which are tangible reminders of ways of life which may now have disappeared.

M Shed, however, is not just about looking back fondly to a golden era. Times were often hard for the workers and the social aspects of manufacturing are covered. Also, M Shed looks at contemporary life in the city where the service industries seem to be replacing the production of actual 'things' and it dares to wonder what the future might hold.

The ambition of the new museum is to update and to change the stories that it tells of real people and their life experiences. To that end it invites you the visitor, whether physically on site or whether at home surfing its website, to contribute your stories of your experiences or of others and to contribute your views on the issues that have confronted, and continue to confront, this great city.

Black beaver felt top hat by D Parsley, 20 Clare Street, Bristol

In the early 1900s, textile trades in Bristol employed more people than any other sector. Bristol's clothing industries remained important until the 1950s, with associated industries such as corsetry and millinery (hat making) being particularly significant

And finally a note about Redcliffe Press

The publishers of this book have now published around 230 books about the city of Bristol – and maybe warrant a little 'write up' of their own. The story began in 1976 when friends and fellow young parents challenged John and Angela Sansom to publish a much needed family guide to Bristol. That iconic little book, *Children's Bristol*, was chosen by Bristol Museums and Art Gallery as an exhibit in the new M Shed Museum. In 2010, *Venue* described the latest edition as 'jaw-droppingly good' and deserving of a civic award.

Since that first success, Redcliffe Press has covered most Bristol topics, from architecture to football, from local cinemas to ghosts in Brislington, and from Bristol's hidden interiors to the city's historic waterfront. A recent departure has been the publication of Tim Mowl's acclaimed county-by-county series on the country's historic gardens.

Over the years, the Sansom family have widened their publishing activities, with imprints specialising in Modern British art, but their core interest remains publishing books about Bristol, for which they have received The Lord Mayor's Medal and *Bristol Evening Post*'s Business Life Time Achievement Award. In July 2011, John Sansom received a doctorate of letters from the University of Bristol for services to publishing and to Bristol.

The story is told in *Written Between the Lines: A Memoir of Redcliffe Press* by John Sansom.

For more information about books in print, please visit:

www.redcliffepress.co.uk
www.sansomandcompany.co.uk
www.artdictionaries.com

Redcliffe books of related interest

Bristol's Floating Harbour: The First 200 Years
Peter Malpass and Andy King

On 1 May, 1809 the port of Bristol was transformed for ever by the completion of the Floating Harbour.

For centuries, ships coming up the Avon had been stranded on the muddy bed of the river at low tide. William Jessop's system of dams and locks kept ships afloat at the quaysides at all times, while a new course for the river Avon (the New Cut) provided a tidal bypass. This massive civil engineering project took five years to complete and cost twice the original estimates, but it improved the efficiency of the port and allowed the City Docks to thrive until the 1960s.

Today the Floating Harbour remains an important and iconic feature of the city. No longer a working port it has been transformed into a place of new apartments, office jobs, leisure and tourism. Peter Malpass and Andy King tell the story of the Floating Harbour from the earliest proposals right through to the present day – drawing on original research and the huge collection of paintings and photographs held in the City's collections. Profusely illustrated in colour and black and white with paintings and atmospheric photographs of the city docks at work.

ISBN 978-1-906593-28-5   160 pages   softback   £14.99

Discovering Harbourside: A journey to the heart of Bristol
James Russell with photographs by Stephen Morris

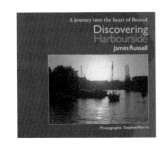

The transformation of Bristol's ancient harbour into the modern Harbourside – the latest chapter in a long and eventful story – is almost complete.

Discovering Harbourside tells this story, more a guide book for time-travellers than a conventional history. Starting with a re-enactment of John Cabot's return to Bristol from Newfoundland in 1497, it brings Bristol's port to life in new and entertaining ways, encouraging readers to look at the city around them and imagine moments, scenes and characters from the city's past. With one eye on the present and the other on the past, the author walks and cycles around the Floating Harbour and down the Avon, looking for clues and retelling stories – some familiar and others new. Did Bristol fishermen discover America before Columbus? What was life at sea like in the age of exploration? How did the Llandoger Trow get its name?

Pirates loom large, with an account of Blackbeard's startling career and violent last battle, and so do more respectable sea captains, from Woodes Rogers to Captain Smith, hero of the Atlantic convoys of World War II. There are disasters and triumphs, from the wreck of the *Demerara* to the return of the ss *Great Britain*.

Discovering Harbourside is both action-packed and thought-provoking. Bristol will never seem quite the same again.

ISBN 978-1-906593-31-5   176 pages   softback   £14.95

Mr Hilhouse of Bristol: Shipbuilder for the Navy 1749-1822
Andrew Whitefield

James Martin Hilhouse (1749-1822) was Bristol's foremost shipbuilder. He built warships for the Navy where none had been built for 100 years and at a time when ships were of vital importance in war and in trade he built privateers for Bristol's enterprising merchants and fast running armed ships for plantation owners and traders. Aged 23 he established in 1773 his company which developed through the age of steam and iron and continued to flourish for the next two centieseeee. In his lifetime he enjoyed a national reputation and yet this man's contribution to Bristol's maritime history has been largely overlooked.

Andrew Whitefield sets out to rediscover Hilhouse's career and answer the questions that first attracted him to the enigma of Hilhouse. How did he start as a first generation shipbuilder? How did he overcome the Navy's prejudice against merchants and reluctance to build at Bristol? Where was his famous Redclift yard? Why did the Navy cease to place orders? Drawing on hitherto unpublished primary sources and following tantalizing clues, he traces Hilhouse's family's origins, their involvement as Dissenters and Merchant Venturers in Bristol's Golden Age trading in sugar and risking all in privateering ventures.

The book describes Hilhouse's shipbuilding career, with details of his dockyard organization, dealings with the Navy and histories of his warships and also recounts the cultural side of his life and influential artistic friends. The story that emerges provides a fascinating portrait of a shipbuilder, artist and family man, during a vital period of Britain's maritime history and gives James Martin Hilhouse the recognition he deserves.

ISBN 978-1-904537-68-1   184 pages   softback   £15.99

From Bristol to the Sea: Artists, the Avon Gorge and Bristol Harbour
Francis Greenacre

This superbly illustrated book is a celebration of how artists have responded to the finest approach to an inland harbour in the world. It illustrates both Bristol's rich maritime heritage and the unsurpassed collection of paintings, watercolours and drawings in Bristol Museum & Art Gallery.

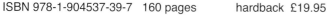

The journey from the heart of the old city to the Bristol Channel is chronological as well as topographical, spanning three hundred years from 1671 to 1995. At the book's core is the famous Bristol School of Artists of the 1820s, particularly Francis Danby and Samuel Jackson. Bristol's outstanding marine painters, Nicholas Pocock and Joseph Walter, are well represented and the book concludes with Bristol's world-famous contemporary artist, Richard Long. Visiting artists are included, from an anonymous itinerant artist of the early eighteenth century, to JMW Turner, John Sell Cotman and the twentieth-century watercolours of John and Paul Nash.

ISBN 978-1-904537-39-7   160 pages   hardback £19.95

Bristol Cranes
Thomas Rasche

Discover the cranes of Bristol! The cranes that can be seen on the quays of Bristol tell a fascinating story. Cranes featured in Bristol from the earliest days. They have changed with time, technology and with the growing city. They were there when the floating harbour was being constructed through the port's heyday and now just a remaining handful stand witness to the city's great maritime past. Thomas Rasche takes you on a memorable journey of discovery.

ISBN 978-1-906593-54-4   40 pages   softback   £5.99

Brunel's Bristol
Angus Buchanan and Michael Williams

The remarkable Isambard Kingdom Brunel made a greater contribution to the landscape of the Bristol area than any other single individual before or since.

Few would argue with Angus Buchanan's judgement: a splendid bridge over the Avon Gorge, a railway network radiating out from Bristol, with Brunel's original Temple Meads station still intact (if put to new uses), the Floating Harbour surviving largely because of the improvements which he introduced, and the s.s. *Great Britain* now handsomely restored in the dry dock from which she was launched in 1843.

This book – the only one to concentrate on Brunel's associations with the city of Bristol – tells of the great engineer's triumphs, exasperations and disappointments in the city which, as a young man, he adopted as his own and which he continued to regard with affection for the rest of his life.

ISBN 978-1-904537-35-9   112 pages   softback   £9.95

Bristol's 100 Best Buildings
Mike Jenner with photographs by Stephen Morris

Architect Mike Jenner sets himself a seemingly impossible task: to choose Bristol's 100 'best' buildings from the Middle Ages to the present day. We can all admire St Mary Redcliffe church and John Wood's Corn Street masterpiece. But, having chosen an obvious handful of great buildings, how does one then go on to rate the Georgian elegance of the city's great terraces and squares against the polychromatic exuberance of Bristol Byzantine? How decide which is 'better': the imposing Arts and Crafts Downleaze, tile-hung and multi-gabled, or the 1930s Connell Ward & Lucas's severe Concrete House in Brentry? Or choose between the delicious Art Nouveau frontage of a former teashop on College Green and the calm and repose of a seventeeth-century almshouse on St Michael's Hill?

This is, of course, a very personal choice, and the point of this entertaining and controversial book is to get people looking, talking and arguing about Bristol's built environment. Mike Jenner reminds us that, outside London, Bristol has a far wider, and more varied, range of building types from all periods than any other town or city in the country. Only by cherishing the best of the past can we hope to encourage excellence in the future.

The author's sparkling commentaries are beautifully complemented by Stephen Morris's superlative photography.

ISBN 978-1-906593-61-2 160 pages   softback   £17.95

Slavery Obscured: The Social History of the Slave Trade in Bristol
Madge Dresser

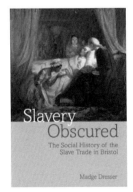

Slavery Obscured is a new departure in the growing history of the impact of the Atlantic slave trade. It aims to assess how the slave trade affected the social life and cultural outlook of the citizens of a major English city, and contends that its impact was more profound than has previously been acknowledged. For much of the eighteenth century, Bristol was England's second city and, between 1730 and 1745, its premier slaving port. Based on original research in archives in Britain and America, *Slavery Obscured* builds on recent scholarship in the economic history of the slave trade to ask questions about the way slave-derived wealth underpinned the city's urban development and its growing gentility.

The author seeks to shed new light on the contradictory and complex history of an English slaving port and, by so doing, to prompt new ways of looking at British national identity, race and history.

ISBN 978-1-904537-69-4   256 pages   softback   £12.95

Pero: The Life of a slave in eighteenth-century Bristol
Christine Eicklemann and David Small

The story of Pero's life as a servant in Nevis and in Bristol and, at a time when the black population in England totalled perhaps 15,000, the authors research throws light on how the eighteenth-century master and black servant relationships worked in practice

ISBN 978-1-904537-03-8   64 pages   softback   £6.99

Douglas Light Aero Engines: From Kingswood to Cathcart
Brian Thorby

This ground-breaking book tells of the contribution made by converted Douglas motorcycle engines to the development of private flying, in the golden age of civil aviation from 1923 to 1939. The story begins in the early 1920s, with prize competitions in Britain and Germany designed to encourage the development of affordable light aircraft. Before the established aero-engine makers took this new market seriously, a major power source was the renowned twin-cylinder motorcycle units made by Douglas, of Kingswood, Bristol.

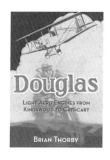

Later, from those Douglas works came Cyril G Pullin, a brilliant designer whose ideas put him among world leaders in rotary-winged aircraft development after he moved to G & J Weir at Cathcart in Glasgow in 1933. Another ex-Douglas engineer, forgotten until now, designed the innovative power units for these autogiros and helicopters. Back in Bristol, some amazing new air-cooled engines were being schemed, until the Kingswood Works were retooled for war work. This profusely illustrated record of a remarkable period in aviation history charts the fortunes of Douglas and its successors, their engines and the aircraft they powered.

ISBN 978-1-906593-25-4   232 pages   softback   £16.95

Bristol Railway Stations
Mike Oakley

This survey of Bristol's branch railway stations and halts by a noted railway historian builds on the author's long out-of-print earlier book, *Bristol Suburban*, updating it where fresh material has become available and including many new photographs. It will appeal to railway enthusiasts as well as anyone interested in Bristol's social, economic and industrial history. Brunel's great Temple Meads terminus is well covered, along with a further twenty-five stations and halts inside the city boundaries which have served residents and commercial interests over the years. A particular feature is the inclusion of a number of 'then and now' photographs.

ISBN 978-1-904537-54-0   112 pages   softback   £9.95

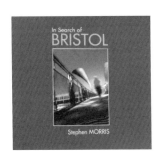

In Search of Bristol
Stephen Morris

Stephen Morris explores the iconic and obscure of his adopted home. *In Search of Bristol* not only celebrates the city's defining vistas – St Mary Redcliffe, Harbourside, the great Clifton terraces – it also roots around some lesser known, but much loved corners. Bristolians who thought they knew their city will be surprised, and delighted. Visitors will want to come again. This is a Bristol to discover and enjoy, with its rich history, its eccentricities and its surprises.

More than 180 photographs in full colour, with commentary, 128 pages

softback: ISBN 978-1-904537-60-1   £10
hardback: ISBN 978-1-904537-59-5   £14.95

Sailing Pilots of the Bristol Channel
Peter Stuckey

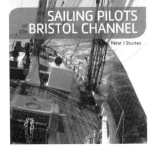

This new printing of Peter Stuckey's classic book on the sailing pilot cutters of the Bristol Channel is a response to public demand.

The author tells of the pilots, westernmen, 'men-in-the-boats' and apprentices from first-hand accounts, with vivid descriptions of the rigours of their daily life afloat and their often incredible feats of seamanship. Generations of men and boats from Bristol, Newport, Barry, Cardiff and Swansea are all commemorated.

In their day they ranged far and wide seeking 'downalong' for ships to pilot from Bristol to Liverpool, off the south coast of Ireland and from fifty miles south-east of Land's End to Start Point in the English Channel. This is their remarkable story, from the earliest days of the Bristol Channel pilotage service to their replacement by steam cutters in the early twentieth century. There are chapters on the craft themselves, how and by whom they were built, along with descriptive appendices on the surprising number of cutters still in commission as prized yachts, museum preservation projects and the growing number of ship's modellers recreating classic craft like the *Cariad* and *Marguerite*.

ISBN 978-1-906593-64-3   184 pages   softback   £27.95